ACHIEV LEVEL

MATHEMATICS

By **Richard Cooper** and **Shirley Armer**

RISING STARS

Rising Stars UK Ltd, 76 Farnaby Road, Bromley, BR1 4BH
www.risingstars-uk.com

Every effort has been made to trace copyright holders and obtain their permission for the use of copyright material. The authors and publishers will gladly receive information enabling them to rectify any error or omission in subsequent editions.

All facts are correct at time of going to press.

Published 2002
New Edition 2002
Reprinted 2002
New Edition 2003
Reprinted 2004
Text, design and layout © Rising Stars UK Ltd.

Editorial: Tanya Solomons
Design: Ken Vail Graphic Design, Cambridge
Illustrations: Burville Riley, Beehive Illustration (Theresa Tibbetts) and
Ken Vail Graphic Design
Cover photo: Amos Morgan/Getty Images
Cover design: Burville Riley

British Library Cataloguing in Publication Data
A CIP record for this book is available from the British Library.

ISBN: 1-904591-07-8

Printed by Wyndeham Gait, Grimsby, UK.

Contents

How to use this book

What we have included:

★ Those topics at Level 4 that are trickiest to get right.
★ All Level 5 content so you know that you are covering all the topics that you need to understand in order to achieve a Level 5.

(1) Introduction – This section tells you what you need to do to get to Level 5. It picks out the key learning objective and explains it simply to you.

(2) Self assessment – Colour in the face that best describes your understanding of this concept.

(3) Question – The question helps you to learn by doing. It is presented in a similar way to a SATs question and gives you a real example to work with.

(4) Flow chart – This shows you the steps to use when completing questions like this. Some of the advice appears on every flow chart (read the question then read it again). This is because this is the best way of getting good marks in the test.

This icon indicates the section is a *teaching* section.

(5) Tip boxes – These provide test hints and general tips on the topic.

Decimals

Achieve 😊 😐 ②

To achieve Level 5 you must be able to work wi[...] [...]ers to two decimal places. Decimals are easy – remember, [...] written with decimals! For example, £9.85 is nearly £10.00; 3.0[...] is a bit more than 3.

Let's practise!

① Wr[...] [...]e missing number.

3.5[...] [...] =

① Read the question then read it again.

② Picture the numbers. What do they look like?

③ Study the numbers again and think [...] about them!

④ When multiplying and dividing, remove the decimal point and calculate.

⑤ Check back to your estimate at Step 3.

⑥ Replace the decimal point.

⑦ Round up or down so you only have 2 numbers after the decimal point.

⑧ If your answer looks sensible, write it in the box.

$3.51 \times 4.9 = ?$

3.51 is around halfway between 3 and 4. 4.9 is just less than 5.

You know the answer is going to be more than 12 (3×4) and less than 20 (4×5). Remember there is a total of three numbers to the right of the decimal points.

$$\begin{array}{r} 351 \\ \times\ \ 49 \\ \hline 3159 \\ 14040 \\ \hline 17199 \end{array}$$

You know that your number is going to be between 12 and 20 (see Step 3).

Count three in from the right (see Step 3). Your answer is 17.199!

17.199 becomes 17.20 when you round to two decimal places.

If it doesn't look right, go back to Step 3 and try again.

★ **Tip 1**

When rounding, remember 5 is always UP!

1.265 = 1.27

★ **Tip 2**

When writing money remember:
£0.45p (✗)   £0.45 (✓)
0.45p (✗)   45p (✓)
Say the answer to yourself before you write it down!

Here is another 'decimals' question we can try together. There are some questions at the bottom of the page for you to try on your own!

Let's practise!

$(6.73 - 4.89) + 1.25 =$ ☐

① Read the question then read it again.

② Picture the numbers. What do they look like?

③ Study the numbers again an[...] about them!

④ Calculate.

⑤ Check back to your estimate at Step 3.

⑥ Make sure your decimal point is in the right place.

⑦ Round up or down so you only have two numbers after the decimal point.

⑧ If your answer looks sensible, write it in the box.

$(6.73 - 4.89) + 1.25 = ?$

6.73 is getting close to 7.
4.89 is nearly 5.
1.25 is a bit more than 1.

$7 - 5 = 2$
$2 + 1$ and a bit = 3 and a bit

Remember – always do the bits in brackets first!
i) $\begin{array}{r} 6.73 \\ -\ 4.89 \\ \hline 1.84 \end{array}$ ii) $\begin{array}{r} 1.84 \\ +\ 1.25 \\ \hline 3.09 \end{array}$

You know that your number is going to be a bit more than 3 (see Step 3 above).

Your answer is 3.09!

You only have two numbers after the decimal point so you don't need to do anything!

If it doesn't, go back to Step 3 and try again.

Practice questions

Here are some questions for you to try. Remember to use the step-by-step app[...] [...]ve. Write your answers to two decimal places.

① $(2.3 + 4.75) \times 5.91 =$ ☐

② £20 − (£4.62 × 3) = ☐

③ $(4.8 + 7.36) \times 6.50 =$ ☐

④ £38 − (£2.55 × 7) = ☐

⑥ **Second question** – On most pages there will be a second question. This will either look at a slightly different question type or give you another example to work through.

⑦ **Practice questions** – This is where you have to do the work! Try each question using the technique in the flow chart then check your answers at the back. Practising questions is the best way to help improve your understanding.

GOOD LUCK!

Achieve Level 5 Maths – Objectives

This chart allows you to see which objectives in the National Numeracy Strategy have been covered and which are to be completed.

We have matched the objectives directly with each page of Achieve Level 5 so you can monitor progress.

When children have indicated 'achievement', you can encourage them to tick the box or highlight that row in this table. That way, you and your class know what has been achieved and what is still to be covered.

Text in **bold** denotes key objectives.

Page no.	Title	Objective	Achieved? (tick)
Level 4 – The Tricky Bits			
8	Predicting sequences	Recognise and extend number sequences formed by counting from any number in steps of constant size, extending beyond zero when counting back (Numbers and the Number System)	
9	Calculators	Develop calculator skills and use a calculator effectively (Calculations)	
10	Perimeter	Measure and calculate the perimeter of rectangles and other simple shapes, using counting methods and standard units (Measures)	
11	The 24 hour clock	Use units of time; read the time on a 24 hour digital clock and use 24 hour clock notation, such as 19:53 (Measures)	
12	Reading	Record estimates and readings from scales to a suitable degree of accuracy (Measures)	
13	Venn diagrams	Solve a problem by collecting quickly, organising, representing and interpreting data in Venn diagrams (Handling Data)	
The Number System and Calculations			
14–15	Checking you answers	Check with the inverse operation Estimate by approximating (round to the nearest 10 or a 100), then check result	
16–17	Multiplying and dividing by 10, 100 and 1000	**Multiply and divide decimals mentally by 10 or 100 and integers by 1000, and explain the effect**	
18–19	Decimals	Extend written methods to short multiplication/division of numbers involving decimals Extend written methods to column addition and subtraction of numbers involving decimals Use brackets	
18–19	Reducing a fraction to its simplest form	**Reduce a fraction to its simplest form by cancelling common factors in the numerator and denominator** **Solve simple problems involving ratio and proportion**	
22–23	Calculating fractions or percentages	**Use a fraction as an 'operator' to find fractions,** including tenths and hundredths, **of numbers or quantities** Develop calculator skills and use a calculator effectively **Find simple percentages of small whole-number quantities**	

Page no.	Title	Objective	Achieved? (tick)
24–25	Multiplication and division	Extend written methods to long multiplication of a three digit by a two digit integer; division of HTU by TU Derive quickly: division facts corresponding to tables up to 10×10 Approximate first. Use informal pencil and paper methods to support record or explain multiplications or divisions	
26–27	Negative numbers	Find the difference between a positive and negative integer, or two negative integers, in a context such as temperature or the number line, and order a set of negative integers	
28–29	Simple formulae	Develop from explaining a generalised relationship in words to expressing it in a formula using letters as symbols	
30–31	Using brackets	Understand and use the relationships between the four operations and the principles (not the names) of the arithmetic laws Use brackets	
Measures, Shape and Space			
32–34	Coordinates	**Read and plot coordinates in all four quadrants**	
35–39	Angles	**Use a protractor to measure and draw angles to the nearest degree** Calculate angles in a triangle or around a point	
40–43	Symmetries of 2D shapes	Recognise where a shape will be after reflection: in a mirror line touching the shape at a point; in two mirror lines at right angles Recognise where a shape will be after two translations	
44–45	Units of measure	Use, read and write standard metric units (km, m, cm, mm, kg, g, l, ml, cl), including their abbreviations, and relationships between them **Convert smaller to larger units and vice versa** **Identify and use appropriate operations (including combinations of operations) to solve word problems involving numbers and quantities based on 'real life', money or measures** Know rough equivalents of lb kg, oz and g, miles and km, litres and pints or gallons	
46–47	Estimating measures	Suggest suitable units and measuring equipment to estimate or measure length, mass or capacity	
48–49	The area of a rectangle	Understand area measured in square centimetres (cm^2) **Understand and use the formula in words 'length × breadth' for the area of a rectangle** **Calculate the area of simple compound shapes that can be split into rectangles**	
Handling Data			
50–51	Finding the mean Finding the median	Begin to find the median and mean of a set of data	
52–53	Finding the range Finding the mode	Find the mode and range of a set of data	
54–55	Graphs and pie charts	**Solve a problem by** representing, **extracting and interpreting data in graphs, charts** and diagrams, including those generated by computer, for example: line graphs for distance/time and conversions	
56–57	The probability scale	Use the language associated with probability to discuss events, including those with equally likely outcomes	

Predicting sequences

This is not as difficult as it sounds. Sequences and patterns just can't live without each other!

Just remember: sequence = numbers following a pattern.

Pattern 1

The pattern may mean the difference between numbers is always the same:

2   4   6   8   10
   +2   +2   +2   +2

Pattern 2

The pattern may mean the difference between numbers changes according to a rule:

5   11   23   41   65
   +6   +12   +18   +24

Let's practise!

Predict the next two numbers in this sequence:
3, 14, 25, 36, __, __

1 Read the question then read it again.

2 Study the numbers.

3 Test the pattern.

4 Does the sequence work? If so, write in the next two numbers.

What is the pattern?

What is the difference between the numbers?

$3 + ? = 14$ $? = 11$
$14 + ? = 25$ $? = 11$

Is the difference between all the numbers 11?

3   14   25   36   47   58
   +11   +11   +11   +11   +11

Yes, the pattern works and the next numbers in the sequence are 47 and 58.

Practice questions

Find the missing numbers in these sequences.

1 23, 31, 39, 47, __, __

2 27, 18, 9, __, __, −18, −27

3 15, 28, 41, 54, __, __

★ Tip 1

You will see the pattern more easily if you write in the numbers underneath the sequence.

4   14   34   64
   +10   +20   +30

★ Tip 2

A sequence may be shown in pictures. Just turn the pictures into numbers to help you see the pattern.

★   ★★   ★★   ★★★★
              ★★   ★★★

It can be written as:

1   2   4   7
   +1   +2   +3

Calculators

Calculators can be seen as the answer to everything in Maths. If used correctly they are a useful tool but when used incorrectly they can become a nightmare!

There are a number of steps you can follow to succeed with calculators.

1 Read the question then read it again.

Does the question need a calculator? Can you work out the question in your head?

2 Press the keys carefully and methodically.

Think clearly. Talk through the calculation in your mind.

3 Check the calculator display

Always check to see if you have pressed the right buttons.

4 Make sure you press the equals key (=) after each calculation.

Do not forget to do this!

5 Does your final answer look sensible? If not, go back to Step 1.

If you feel the need to redo a calculation, don't hold back. A couple of seconds redoing a sum could save you a couple of marks!

Practice questions

Try these sums on your calculator.

1 $951 + 357 =$

2 $101 - 1.1 =$

3 $963 \div 12 =$

4 $87 \times 6.7 =$

5 $524 \times 5.24 =$

6 $707 \div 0.07 =$

★ Tip 1

Don't forget to press the decimal point key when keying in decimal numbers.

$3.5 =$ **3** **.** **5**

★ Tip 2

As you press each button, check to see what appears on the display.

Perimeter

Achieved?
☺ 😐 ☹

Let's look at how to calculate the perimeter of a shape.

A common mistake is to forget one side of a shape when measuring it!

KEY FACT
The perimeter is the total distance around the outside of a shape.

Let's practise!

What is the perimeter of this shape?

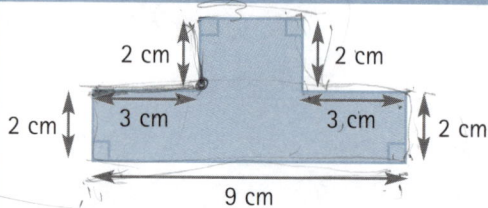

2 cm   2 cm

2 cm   3 cm   3 cm   2 cm

9 cm

1 Read the question then read it again.

What are we being asked to do? We are being asked to measure the distance around the shape.

2 Choose a side to start from. Put a line through it with your pencil.

This helps you to remember where you started from.

3 Add up all the lengths that are given in the question. Mark them off as you go.

2 cm + 3 cm + 2 cm + 2 cm + 3 cm + 2 cm + 9 cm = 23 cm

4 Now work out the lengths of the sides you haven't been given.

This is the IMPORTANT PART!
The right angles show you that the distance along the top of the shape must be the same as the distance along the bottom. Both must be **9 cm**.

The missing side must be 3 cm because 3 cm + **3 cm** + 3 cm is **9 cm**

5 Add the missing length to the total of the lengths you have been given (see Step 3).

23 cm + 3 cm = 26 cm

6 Is your answer a sensible one? If so, put it in the box.

The perimeter of the shape is 26 cm.

★ Tip 1

Think of a perimeter fence going all the way round a football pitch.

★ Tip 2

Don't try to measure 'missing' sides with a ruler. The reason they are missing is because the test wants to see if you can work it out from the given lengths.

The 24 hour clock

Achieved?
☺ 😐 ☹

You should be pretty good at telling the time by now but certain questions can still cause problems. It is very easy to make silly mistakes when dealing with the 24 hour clock. When you are working out time it is important to take things step-by-step.

18.23

Let's practise!

How long is it from 01:12 to 22:15?

1. Read the question then read it again.

2. Picture the question.

Imagine the times – 01:12 is very early in the morning; 22:15 is late at night. The answer is going to be quite high.

3. Count the minutes round to the first hour.

01:12 to 02:00 is 48 minutes.

4. Now count the hours round to the given hour.

2:00 to 22:00 is 20 hours.

5. Add up the minutes and convert to hours if you need to.

48 minutes + the 15 minutes from the time 22:15 = 63 minutes.
63 minutes = 1 hour and 3 minutes.

6. Calculate all the hours and add the remaining minutes to give a final answer.

20 hours + 1 hour + 3 minutes = 21 hours and 3 minutes.

7. Does the answer look sensible? If so, put it in the box.

Yes. 21 hours and 3 minutes is correct.

Practice questions

Work out the following times in hours and minutes.

1. 09:46 to 15:38 _____

2. 07:28 to 18:55 _____

3. 19:41 to 02:27 _____

4. 22:08 to 23:53 _____

★ Tip 1

Get used to reading timetables for buses, trains and aeroplanes. Test yourself on imaginary journeys.

★ Tip 2

Remember, when comparing times the **fastest** one is the **shortest** one.

Reading scales

We use scales to measure things. They are just like number lines! The tricky bit is remembering that you need to work out what each mark on the scale stands for.

Let's practise!

How much water is there in the measuring cylinder? [   ] ml

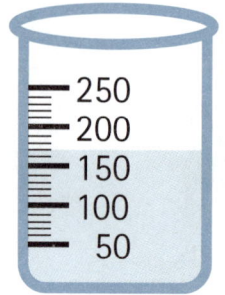

- 250
- 200
- 150
- 100
- 50

1 Read the question then read it again.

2 Picture the numbers.

3 Study the scale.

The answer is between 150 ml and 200 ml.

Count the gaps made by the small lines between 150 ml and 200 ml. There are 5 gaps. We therefore know that **5 gaps must equal 50 ml**.

4 Calculate the scale.

5 gaps = 50 ml
1 gap = 10 ml (50 ÷ 5)

5 Answer the question.

Water level is at 150 ml plus 2 gaps
= 150 ml + 20 ml
= 170 ml

6 If your answer looks sensible, write it in the box.

If not, go back to Step 2 and try again.

Practice questions

How much water is in these measuring cylinders?

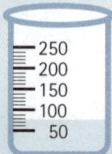

1
- 250
- 200
- 150
- 100
- 50

[   ]

2
- 250
- 200
- 150
- 100
- 50

[   ]

★ Tip 1

Read scales very carefully and count the gaps more than once to be sure you have got it right. Write in missing measurements in pencil to help you remember them.

★ Tip 2

Always check your answer carefully to be sure it makes sense.

Venn diagrams

Venn diagrams may sound complicated but really they are just a way of sorting information into groups. Look at the diagram. There are three regions – A, B and C.

Region A belongs to group A.
Region B belongs to group B.
Region C belongs to group A and group B.

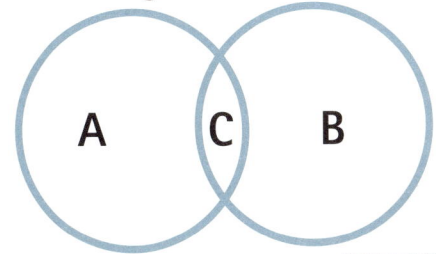

Let's practise!

Look at this table and sort the names into the sorting diagram. Decide on a description for each region.

Name	Likes apples	Likes bananas
Mary	✔	✗
Jack	✗	✔
Fabio	✔	✔
Ronnie	✔	✔
Sarah	✔	✗
Gemma	✔	✗
Joshua	✔	✗

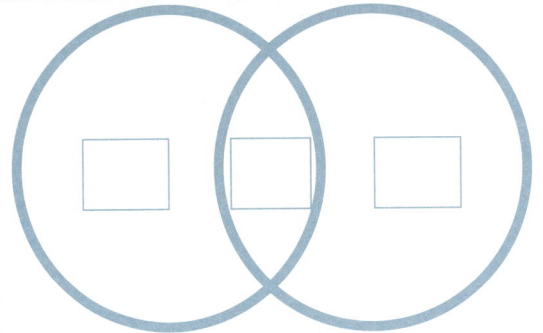

1 Read the question then read it again.

We need to sort the names into groups and decide on definitions or labels for each of these groups.

2 Study the information given.

We can sort the information into two main groups: Group A (children who like apples) and Group B (children who like bananas).

Group C will therefore be children who like apples and bananas.

3 Sort the information.

Write out the groups on practice paper first.

4 Check your answer against your table.

Check back to make sure you have included all the children in the right groups before completing your answer.

Checking your answers

Achieved? 🙂 😐 🙁

Inverse operations

Remember, adding and subtracting are OPPOSITES. Multiplying and dividing are OPPOSITES. We can use this knowledge to check our calculations quickly.

| e.g. | $75 + 85 = 160$ | CHECK | $160 - 85 = 75$ |
| or | $42 \times 6 = 252$ | CHECK | $252 \div 6 = 42$ |

INVERSE means the same as OPPOSITE

Let's practise!

$2128 \div 28 = \boxed{}$

1 Read the question then read it again.

Divide 2128 by 28.

2 Study the numbers. Picture them in your head.

Picture them on a number line.

3 Perform the calculation.

$$\begin{array}{r} 76 \\ 28\overline{)2128} \\ \underline{196} \\ 168 \end{array}$$

4 Does the answer look sensible? If it does, check it using the INVERSE OPERATION.

The opposite of dividing is multiplying so...

$$\begin{array}{r} 76 \\ \times\quad 28 \\ \hline 608 \\ \underline{1520} \\ \underline{2128} \end{array}$$

5 Does the check answer match the original sum? If it does, enter the answer in the box! If it doesn't, go back to Step 1.

Yes! Our answer is correct!

Practice questions

Do these calculations and then check your answers using the inverse operation.

1 $92 \times 36 = \boxed{}$

2 $471 + 849 = \boxed{}$

3 $13\ 662 \div 23 = \boxed{}$

4 $8076 - 591 = \boxed{}$

⭐ **Tip**

Get into the habit of checking your answers. It may help you do better in your test!

Rounding up or down

Another excellent way to check your answers is to round the numbers in the question up or down. Doing this will give you a simple sum to do and give you a rough answer.

Let's practise!

$52 \times 28 = \boxed{}$

1 Read the question then read it again.

$52 \times 28 = ?$

2 Study the numbers. Picture them in your head.

Picture them on a number line.

3 Perform the calculation.

$$\begin{array}{r} 52 \\ \times\ \ 28 \\ \hline 416 \\ 1040 \\ \hline 1456 \end{array}$$

4 Now round off the numbers and mentally calculate your answer.

52 ROUND TO 50
28 ROUND TO 30
$50 \times 30 = 1500$

5 Are the answers reasonably close? If so, enter your answer in the box. If not, you must go back to Step 1.

Yes, 1456 is pretty close to 1500. Our answer looks correct!

Practice questions

Do these calculations and then check your answers using the 'Rounding Up or Down' technique.

1 $88 \times 71 = \boxed{}$

2 $4607 - 395 = \boxed{}$

3 $796 - 507 = \boxed{}$

4 $782 \div 17 = \boxed{}$

★ Tip 1

When rounding up or down think of 'friendly' numbers. These are numbers you can work with easily in your head. Some examples are 2, 5, 10, 50, 100 and so on.

★ Tip 2

Get used to doing mental calculations every day. Give your brain 'gym exercises' to do which involve calculating numbers quickly. Darts can be a fun way to do this!

Multiplying and dividing by 10, 100 and 1000

At Level 5 you must be able to multiply and divide whole numbers and decimals by 10, 100 and 1000.

Let's practise!

Write in the missing number.

$4.73 \times 10 = $ ☐

1. Read the question then read it again.

2. Picture the numbers. What do they look like?

3. Study the numbers again and think about them.

4. Remember the rules!

5. Calculate.

6. Check your answer.

7. If your answer looks sensible, write it in the box. If not, go back to Step 3.

$4.73 \times 10 = $

4.73 is nearly 5.

You know the answer should be about 50 $(5 \times 10 = 50)$.

To multiply a decimal by 10 shuffle the numbers one place to the left, leaving the decimal point in place.

4.73×10 Shift the numbers one place to the left.

so $4.73 \times 10 = 47.3$
47.3 is nearly 50

From Step 3 we know our answer should be about 50. Our answer looks correct!

KEY FACTS – Multiplication

★ To multiply a decimal by 100, shuffle the numbers two places to the left.

★ To multiply a decimal by 1000, shuffle the numbers three places to the left.

★ Sometimes you will need to add zeros to fill blank spaces.
e.g. $3.8 \times 100 = 380$
$2.68 \times 1000 = 2680$

★ Tip

When multiplying whole numbers by 10, 100 and 1,000, just add the correct number of zeros!

× 10	add 0 to the end	$27 \times 10 = 270$
× 100	add 00 to the end	$27 \times 100 = 2700$
× 1000	add 000 to the end	$27 \times 1000 = 27\,000$

Let's try another question. This time we will DIVIDE a decimal number. (Remember: dividing is the opposite of multiplying.)

Let's practise!

Write in the missing number.

$$38.3 \div 10 = \boxed{}$$

① Read the question then read it again.

② Picture the numbers. What do they look like?

③ Study the numbers again and think about them.

④ Remember the rules!

⑤ Calculate.

⑥ Check your answer.

⑦ If your answer looks sensible, write it in the box.
If not go back to Step 3.

$38.3 \div 10 =$

38.3 is nearly 40.

You know the answer should be about 4 $(40 \div 10 = 4)$.

To divide a decimal by 10, shuffle the numbers one place to the right.

Shift the numbers one place to the right.

so $38.3 \div 10 = 3.83$
3.83 is nearly 4

From Step 3 we know our answer should be about 4. Our answer looks correct!

KEY FACTS - Division

★ To divide a decimal by 100, shuffle the numbers **two** places to the right.

★ To divide a decimal by 1000, shuffle the numbers **three** places to the right.

Practice questions

① $37 \times 10 = \boxed{}$

② $42 \times \boxed{} = 4200$

③ $0.3 \times 10 = \boxed{}$

④ $4.6 \div 10 = \boxed{}$

⑤ $362 \div \boxed{} = 36.2$

⑥ $6500 \div 1000 = \boxed{}$

Decimals

Achieved?
☺ 😐 ☹

To achieve Level 5 you must be able to work with numbers to two decimal places. Decimals are easy – remember, money is written with decimals! For example, £9.85 is nearly £10.00; 3.07 is a bit more than 3.

Let's practise!

Write in the missing number.
$3.51 \times 4.9 =$ [   ]

$3.51 \times 4.9 = ?$

1 Read the question then read it again.

2 Picture the numbers. What do they look like?

3.51 is around halfway between 3 and 4. 4.9 is just less than 5.

3 Study the numbers again and think about them!

You know the answer is going to be more than 12 (3 × 4) and less than 20 (4 × 5). Remember there is a total of three numbers to the right of the decimal points.

4 When multiplying and dividing, remove the decimal point and calculate.

```
        351
    ×    49
       3159
      14040
      17199
```

5 Check back to your estimate at Step 3.

You know that your number is going to be between 12 and 20 (see Step 3).

6 Replace the decimal point.

Count three in from the right (see Step 3). Your answer is 17.199!

7 Round up or down so you only have 2 numbers after the decimal point.

17.199 becomes 17.20 when you round to two decimal places.

8 If your answer looks sensible, write it in the box.

If it doesn't look right, go back to Step 3 and try again.

★ Tip 1

When rounding, remember 5 is always UP!

1.265 = 1.27

★ Tip 2

When writing money remember:
£0.45p (✗)   £0.45 (✓)
0.45p (✗)   45p (✓)
Say the answer to yourself before you write it down!

Here is another 'decimals' question we can try together. There are some questions at the bottom of the page for you to try on your own!

Let's practise!

$(6.73 - 4.89) + 1.25 =$ [ ]

1 Read the question then read it again.

$(6.73 - 4.89) + 1.25 = ?$

2 Picture the numbers. What do they look like?

6.73 is getting close to 7.
4.89 is nearly 5.
1.25 is a bit more than 1.

3 Study the numbers again and think about them!

$7 - 5 = 2$
$2 + 1$ and a bit $= 3$ and a bit

4 Calculate.

Remember – always do the bits in brackets first!

i)   6.73
    – 4.89
      1.84

ii)   1.84
    + 1.25
      3.09

5 Check back to your estimate at Step 3.

You know that your number is going to be a bit more than 3 (see Step 3 above).

6 Make sure your decimal point is in the right place.

Your answer is 3.09!

7 Round up or down so you only have two numbers after the decimal point.

You only have two numbers after the decimal point so you don't need to do anything!

8 If your answer looks sensible, write it in the box.

If it doesn't, go back to Step 3 and try again.

Practice questions

Here are some questions for you to try.
Remember to use the step-by-step approach above. Write your answers to two decimal places.

1 $(2.3 + 4.75) \times 5.91 =$ [ ]

3 $(4.8 + 7.36) \times 6.50 =$ [ ]

2   £20 – (£4.62 × 3) = [ ]

4   £38 – (£2.55 × 7) = [ ]

Reducing fractions

Reducing fractions is all about finding a fraction's 'common factors'. For example:

$\frac{4}{6}$ can be reduced to $\frac{2}{3}$ (because 4 and 6 can both be divided by 2)

$\frac{2}{4}$ can be reduced to $\frac{1}{2}$ (because 2 and 4 can both be divided by 2)

Let's practise!

What is $\frac{36}{90}$ in its lowest form?

1 Read the question then read it again.

2 Are both numbers divisible by 2? Yes? Then divide them both by 2. No? Move to Step 4.

Yes $36 \div 2 = 18$
      $90 \div 2 = 45$

3 Look at your new fraction. Can the numbers be divided by 2 again? Yes? Repeat Step 2. No? Move to Step 4.

$\frac{18}{45}$
Both numbers cannot be divided by 2 so we move to Step 4.

4 Study the fraction. Which number (other than 1) can be divided into both the top and bottom numbers?

Both 18 and 45 can be divided by 9!

5 Reduce the fraction. Enter your answer in the box.

$18 \div 9 = 2$ $45 \div 9 = 5$
Our answer is $\frac{2}{5}$

Practice questions

Reduce each of these fractions to their lowest form.

1 $\frac{14}{42} = $ ☐   **2** $\frac{15}{40} = $ ☐   **3** $\frac{36}{48} = $ ☐   **4** $\frac{32}{56} = $ ☐

★ Tip 1

Learn to recognise these equivalent fractions.

$\frac{1}{3} = \frac{2}{6} = \frac{3}{9} = \frac{4}{12} = \frac{5}{15} = \frac{6}{18} = \frac{7}{21}$

$\frac{1}{4} = \frac{2}{8} = \frac{3}{12} = \frac{4}{16} = \frac{5}{20} = \frac{6}{24} = \frac{7}{28}$

$\frac{1}{5} = \frac{2}{10} = \frac{3}{15} = \frac{4}{20} = \frac{5}{25} = \frac{6}{30} = \frac{7}{35}$

★ Tip 2

Remember, when you are reducing a fraction ask yourself the following questions **before writing anything down**:
★ Which numbers fit?
★ How many times do they fit?

You can use your ability to reduce fractions to their lowest form to help you answer questions on RATIO and PROPORTION.

Let's practise!

Have a look at this pattern of squares:

What is the ratio of blue squares to white squares? [ ]

1. Read the question then read it again.

2. Count the number of blue squares. → There are 4 blue squares.

3. Now count the white squares. → There are 8 white squares.

4. What is the ratio of blue squares to white squares? → The ratio is 4:8

5. Can you reduce the ratio? → Follow Step 2 to Step 5 on page 20.

6. Write your answer in the box. → Write this as a ratio 1:2

KEY FACT

When doing a question about proportion, count the TOTAL number of squares. This can be written as a fraction.

The proportion of blue squares in the pattern at the top of this page is 4 in 12 or $\frac{4}{12}$. Reduce this using the steps on page 20. The proportion of blue squares in the whole pattern is 1 in 3 or $\frac{1}{3}$.

Practice questions

Look at the pattern below and answer the following questions:

1. What is the ratio of blue squares to white squares?

2. What is the proportion of blue squares in the whole pattern?

★ Tip

If you are asked to find a **proportion** of two things or numbers you are being asked to find a **fraction** (in its lowest form).

Calculating fractions or percentages

Achieved? 😊 😐 ☹

Without a calculator

Lots of questions that ask you to find fractions or percentages of things are easy to answer WITHOUT a calculator by just using some simple maths, such as doubling, halving or dividing by 10. For example:

70% of 900 metres

10% of 900 is 90

so 70% of 900 is 7×90

$7 \times 90 = 630$

= 630 metres

Let's practise!

A jacket costs £130. In the sales the price is reduced by 15%. What is the new price of the jacket?

1 Read the question then read it again. What am I being asked to do?

Find the NEW price of the jacket.

2 To find the discount, first calculate 10% of the original price.

10% of £130 = £13.

3 Now calculate 5% of the original price and add your answers together to find 15%.

5% is half of 10% so 5% is £6.50
(5%) + (10%) = (15%)
£6.50 + £13.00 = £19.50

4 Don't forget the next part! What is the NEW price of the jacket?

The jacket has been reduced by £19.50
So the new price is £130 – £19.50 = £110.50

5 Check you have answered the question properly.

What is the new price of the jacket? After a discount of £19.50 the new price is £110.50.

⭐ **Tip 1**

To find 1% of something, first find 10% then find 10% of THAT answer. You can work out any % by adding all the 10%, 5% and 1% answers together!

⭐ **Tip 2**

Remember as many percentage/fraction equivalents as you can:

$50\% = \frac{1}{2}$ $25\% = \frac{1}{4}$ $75\% = \frac{3}{4}$

$33\% = $ nearly $\frac{1}{3}$ $66\% = $ nearly $\frac{2}{3}$

With a calculator

You can work out many fractions or percentages very easily without a calculator but sometimes it's not so easy. For example, if you scored 15 out of 30 in your spelling test you should be able to recognise that you got 50% correct. If you improved the following week and got 24 out of 30 then you may need to use your calculator! Calculate as follows:

Key in   24   then   ÷   then   30   then   %

You should have the answer 80, which means you scored 80% correct.

Let's practise!

Calculate 51 out of 68 as a percentage.

1 Read the question then read it again.

2 Picture the numbers in your head.

3 Type in the numbers.

4 Press the % key.

5 Does your answer look sensible? If so, put your answer in the box.

51 out of 68 means $\frac{51}{68}$

51 out of 68 is nearly 50 out of 70 or $\frac{5}{7}$. Our answer will be somewhere between $\frac{1}{2}$ and 1

51   ÷   68

%

Our answer is 75%. Remember it only takes a moment to redo the calculation as a check!

Practice questions

Work these out **without** a calculator.

1 75% of 500 cm ☐   **2** 40% of 160 kg ☐   **3** 35% of £260 ☐

4 65% of 800 ml ☐   **5** 80% of 440 g ☐   **6** 30% of £3330 ☐

Practice questions

Work these out with a calculator (express them as a %).

1 $\frac{48}{150} =$ ☐   **2** $\frac{77}{220} =$ ☐   **3** $\frac{65}{500} =$ ☐   **4** $\frac{270}{360} =$ ☐

Multiplication and division

Achieved? ☺ 😐 ☹

To get a Level 5 you need to be able to multiply and divide a 3-digit number by a 2-digit number without a calculator! EASY!

Let's practise!

Write in the missing number. $217 \times 48 =$ ☐

1. Read the question then read it again.

$217 \times 48 =$

2. Picture the numbers.

217 is close to 200.
48 is close to 50.

3. Study the numbers and think about them.

217×48 is approximately
$200 \times 50 = 10\ 000$

4. Calculate your answer.

$$
\begin{array}{r}
217 \\
\times\ \ 48 \\
\hline
1736 \quad (217 \times 8) \\
8680 \quad (217 \times 40) \\
\hline
10416
\end{array}
$$

5. Does your answer look sensible? If it does then write it in the box. If it doesn't then go back to Step 3.

10 416 is close to 10 000 (see Step 3). Our answer looks sensible!

Write in the missing number. $587 \times 32 =$ ☐

1. Read the question then read it again.

$587 \times 32 =$

2. Picture the numbers.

587 is close to 600.
32 is close to 30.

3. Study the numbers and think about them.

587×32 is approximately
$600 \times 30 = 18\ 000$

4. Calculate your answer.

$$
\begin{array}{r}
587 \\
\times\ \ 32 \\
\hline
1174 \quad (587 \times 2) \\
17610 \quad (587 \times 30) \\
\hline
18784
\end{array}
$$

5. Does your answer look sensible? If it does, write it in the box. If it doesn't, go back to Step 3.

18 784 is approximately 18 000 (see Step 3). Our answer looks sensible!

Now let's try division!

Write in the missing number. 917 ÷ 12 = ☐

1 Read the question then read it again.

917 ÷ 12 =

2 Picture the numbers – what do they look like?

917 is close to 900. 12 is close to 10.

3 Study the numbers and think about them.

917 ÷ 12 is approximately 900 ÷ 10 = 90

4 Calculate your answer.

```
        76.4
   12 )917
        84
        77
        72
        50
        48
```

5 If your answer looks sensible, write it in the box.

Our answer (to one decimal place) is 76.4.

KEY FACT × and ÷ are opposites

Use this fact to help with tricky questions. For example:

21 × 16 = 336   336 ÷ 21 = 16

16 × ☐ = 336   so   336 ÷ 16 = 21   Our missing number is 21.

Practice questions

Try these for practice.

1 486 ÷ 27 = ☐

2 852 ÷ 12 ☐

3 744 ÷ ☐ = 24

4 361 × 35 = ☐

5 792 × 83 = ☐

6 457 × ☐ = 5484

★ Tip

Be neat. Keep your numbers in the right columns.

	WRONG ✗	RIGHT ✓
	312	312
	× 14	× 14
	3120	3120
	1248	1248
	4368	4368

Negative numbers

Achieved?

Be positive! NEGATIVE NUMBERS ARE EASY. Imagine a thermometer and you have a number line with positive and negative numbers. So chill out and try this question.

Let's practise!

Put these temperatures in order from coldest to warmest:

−8°, −20°, −3°, 18°, 30°, 6°, −10°

1   Read the question then read it again.

Negative numbers are colder than positive numbers.

2   Picture the numbers.

Group the numbers.
Negative: (−8°, −20°, −3°, −10°)
Positive: (18°, 30°, 6°)

3   Study the numbers.

Draw a number line. Don't forget to include 'zero'. Decide where each number goes.

−20°   −10°−8° −3° 0°   6°   18°   30°

4   Check your answer.

Are the numbers in order?
Check you have used every number.

5   If your answer looks sensible, write it in the box.

If not go back to Step 3 and try again.

★ Tip 1

Numbers are often called INTEGERS. Don't let this put you off. This just means WHOLE numbers without decimals!

These are integers   1, 2, 3, 4

These are **not** integers   5.6, 7.8, 11.3

★ Tip 2

When thinking of negative (−) numbers,   think of a ladder going into a hole in the ground.

−2 is higher than −6
−2 is a larger number than −6

−5 is below −4
−5 is a smaller number than −4

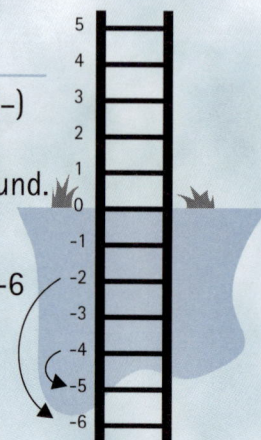

5
4
3
2
1
0
−1
−2
−3
−4
−5
−6

Try another question. This time it's a word problem.

Let's practise!

The temperature is −6°. It rises by 9°.

What is the new temperature?

1 Read the question then read it again.

Rises means **getting warmer**.

2 Picture the numbers.

−6° is colder than 9°.

3 Calculate your answer.

−9 −8 −7 −6 −5 −4 −3 −2 −1 0 1 2 3 4 5 6 7 8 9 10

The temperature starts at -6°. We then need to count up 9 places.

4 Check your answer.

Did you count in the right direction? When adding to a negative number always count to the right on a number line.

5 If your answer checks out, write it in the box.

Our answer is 3° which is 9° warmer than −6°!

−25 −24 −23 −22 −21 −20 −19 −18 −17 −16 −15 −14 −13 −12 −11 −10 −9 −8 −7 −6 −5 −4 −3 −2 −1 −0 1 2 3 4 5 6 7 8 9 10 11 12 13 14 15 16 17 18 19 20 21 22 23 24 25

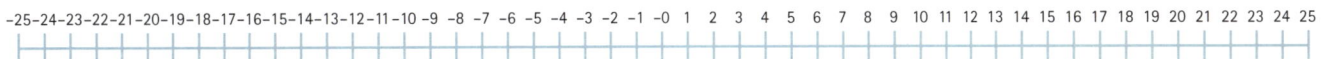

Practice questions

Use the number line to help you.

1 Put these temperatures in order, lowest to highest:

−2°, 3°, 0°, −5°, −7°

2 Order these integers correctly starting with the smallest:

−25, −21, 17, 6, −17

3 At 8am the temperature is −2°. It falls by 3° every hour.

What will the temperature be at 3pm?

4 On Tuesday the temperature was −3°. On Wednesday the temperature was 12°.

What is the difference between Tuesday's and Wednesday's temperatures?

Simple formulae

Formulae can be written in words or in letters. To achieve Level 5 you may be required to make up your own formulae in the tests. This is easier than it sounds! Let's start by working through this example.

Let's practise!

Here is a formula for finding the total cost of some computer games.

$T = £15 \times N$

T = total cost   Each game costs £15   N = number of games

Now write a formula for finding the cost of one game when the total cost of N games is £135 and the cost of one game is C.

1 Read the question then read it again.

Lots to read and think about here!

2 What am I being asked to do?

Write a formula for finding the cost of one game using £135 and 'N'.

3 It will help if you say the formula to yourself.

The total cost is the cost of one game, C, multiplied by the total number of games, N. So...
The cost of one game is the total cost, £135, divided by the total number of games.

4 Change your logical statement into a simple formula. Say it to yourself when you write it down.

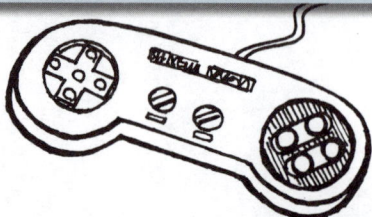

The cost of one game...   C
...is the total cost...   £135
...divided by (÷) the total
number of games   N

$C = 135 \div N$ **OR**
$C = \dfrac{135}{N}$

★ Tip 1

★ Talk through your formula in your head.
★ Think clearly.
★ Take it step-by-step.

★ Tip 2

It helps to only use letters that relate to the information in the question, e.g. **C** = Cost.

A simple formula is often used to find out the total cost of items bought. In words this formula can be written:

"The total cost is the price of one item multiplied by the number of those items bought."

In letter formulae this could be written as: $T = N \times P$

T = total cost   P = price of each item   N = number of items bought

Practice questions

Use the $T = N \times P$ formula to work out these questions.

1   What is the value of **T** if **N** = 6 and **P** = £1.50?

2   What is the value of **N** if **T** = £20 and **P** = £4?

3   What is the value of **P** if **T** = £36 and **N** = 2?

Example question

Andrea and Jamie are playing a number game. Jamie gives Andrea a number which she changes using a rule:

"I take Jamie's number and multiply it by 7 then subtract 2."

Write a formula to show the process Andrea goes through to get to her answer.

Use J for Jamie's number and A for Andrea's answer.

$A = (J \times 7) - 2$

Practice question

Now Andrea changes the rule:

"I take Jamie's number and multiply it by 5 then add 4."

Write a formula to show the process Andrea goes through to get to her answer. Use J for Jamie's number and A for Andrea's answer.

$A =$

★ Tip

If a number and a letter are next to each other, e.g. 4N, it means they are multiplied. Why is the × (multiply) symbol left out? It could get confused with the letter x!!

Using brackets

Achieved?
☺ 😐 ☹

To achieve Level 5 in Maths you must be able to answer questions that contain brackets. Let's look at a simple example.

Firstly, a sum without brackets might look like this:

$5 \times 4 + 7 = 27$

If brackets are used then the answer changes:

$5 \times (4 + 7) = 55$

> **CALCULATIONS INSIDE BRACKETS MUST BE DONE FIRST!**
>
> Our second example actually becomes $5 \times 11 = 55$ when we calculate the brackets first.

Let's practise!

$(673 - 489) \div 23 = \boxed{}$

① Read the question then read it again.

$(673 - 489) \div 23 = ?$

② Picture the numbers. What do they look like?

Picture them on a number line.

③ Calculate the numbers in the brackets first. Check your answer to see if it's sensible.

$$\begin{array}{r} 673 \\ -\ 489 \\ \hline 184 \end{array}$$

④ Complete the calculation and enter your answer.

$$\begin{array}{r} 8 \\ 23\overline{)184} \\ 184 \end{array}$$

★ Tip

Brackets are very sensitive and need your attention.

ALWAYS CALCULATE THE BRACKETS FIRST!

Here is another question with brackets that we can do together. Try the practice questions at the bottom when you think you're ready.

Let's practise!

$$\frac{(48 \times 4) + (154 \times 2)}{20} = \boxed{}$$

1 Read the question then read it again.

$$\frac{(48 \times 4) + (154 \times 2)}{20} = ?$$

2 Picture the numbers. What do they look like?

Picture them on a number line. Is this a big number?

3 Calculate the numbers in the brackets first.

i)
$$\begin{array}{r} 48 \\ \times 4 \\ \hline 192 \end{array}$$

ii)
$$\begin{array}{r} 154 \\ \times 2 \\ \hline 308 \end{array}$$

4 Complete the calculation and then enter the answer.

$192 + 308 = \mathbf{500}$ then

$$\begin{array}{r} 25 \\ 20\overline{)500} \\ 40 \\ \hline 100 \end{array}$$

Practice questions

Here are some questions for you to try. Remember to use the step-by-step approach above.

1 $78 \times (97 + 42) = \boxed{}$

2 $(41 \times 76) + \boxed{} = 4000$

3 $(14 \times 60) + \boxed{} = 850$

4 $\dfrac{(57 \times 6) - (41 \times 7)}{5} = \boxed{}$

Coordinates

☺ 😐 ☹

To achieve Level 5 you should be familiar with coordinates and quadrants. Let's try a question to practise what we know!

Let's practise!

Write down the coordinates of each point on this graph.

1st quadrant = (_ , _)

2nd quadrant = (_ , _)

3rd quadrant = (_ , _)

4th quadrant = (_ , _)

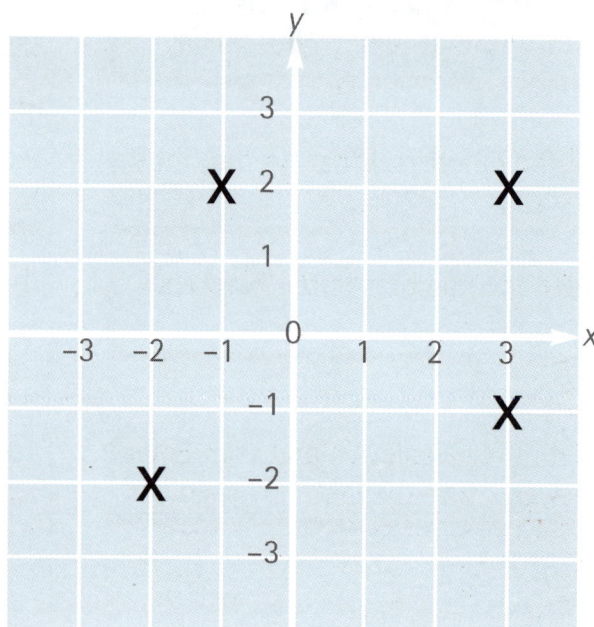

Remember which quadrant is which!

2nd	1st
3rd	4th

1 Read the question then read it again.

2 Practise your answer.

3 Check the number of each quadrant.

You can sketch in lines to help you read the coordinates.

2nd quadrant	*y*	1st quadrant
3rd quadrant		4th quadrant

4 Read off the coordinates in each quadrant.

Remember:
ALONG the *x* axis first then **UP** or **DOWN** the *y* axis

1 (3, 2)   2 (−1, 2)
3 (−2, −2)   4 (3, −1)

5 Double-check and write in your answer.

Check twice! Write once!

Let's try another question.

Draw a reflection of the pentagon in the x axis. Record the coordinates of each vertex.

(_ . _)
(_ . _)
(_ . _)
(_ . _)
(_ . _)

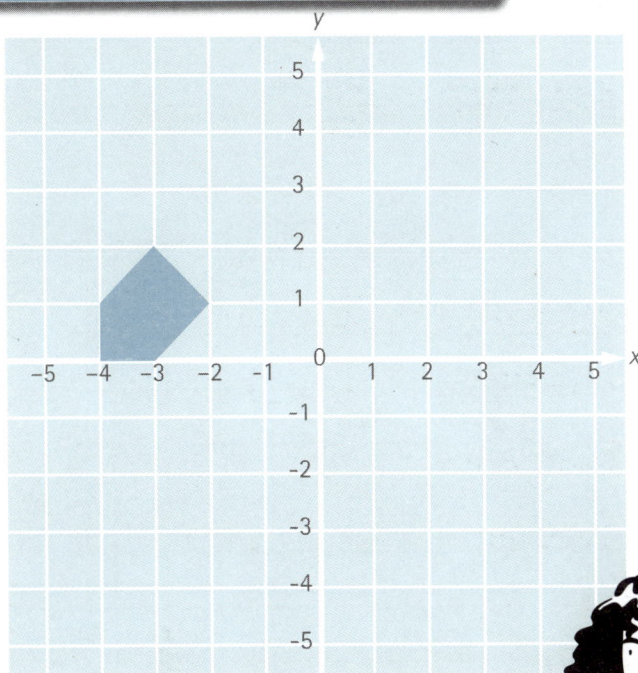

1 Read the question then read it again.

Note you are being asked to work in the 3rd quadrant. 'vertex = corner'

2 Practise your answer.

Sketch your pentagon on rough paper first.

3 Note the position of your shape.

Remember your pentagon must go in the 3rd quadrant!

4 Draw your shape on the grid above.

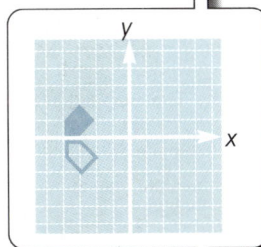

5 Read off your coordinates.

Remember ALONG then UP/DOWN
(-4, 0), (-4, -1), (-3, -2), (-2, -1), (-3, 0)

6 Double-check and write in the answer.

Check twice! Write once!

When you feel comfortable with this, try the practice questions over the page...

Practice questions

1 In which quadrants will we find:

(−3, −2)?   (−2, 1)?   (1, 3)?

[   ]   [   ]   [   ]

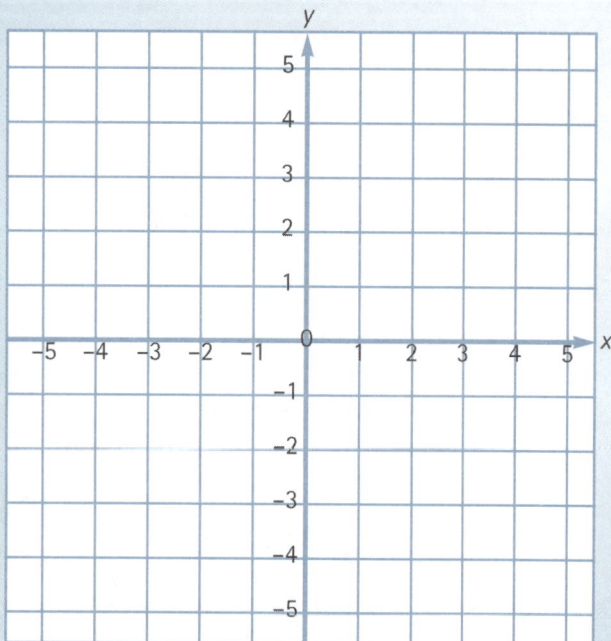

2 Draw a reflection of the parallelogram in the *x* axis. Name the coordinates of the reflected shape.

(__ , __) (__ , __) (__ , __) (__ , __)

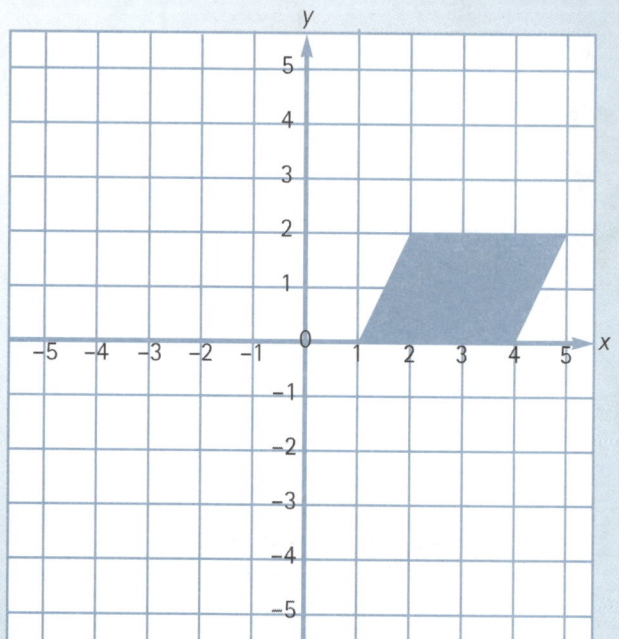

★ Tip 1

Coordinates always go ALONG the corridor and UP the stairs.

But miss, you can go DOWN stairs as well!

Always go along first when reading coordinates. *x* (axis) comes before *y* (axis)!

★ Tip 2

Coordinates are always written in brackets.
(3, 4)   (−3, −2)
or
(*x* axis, *y* axis)

★ Tip 3

The coordinates plot where the grid lines cross, **not** the space in between them.

Angles

Achieved? ☺ 😐 ☹

To achieve Level 5 you will need to be able to measure and draw angles and use the correct language for them.

Measuring angles

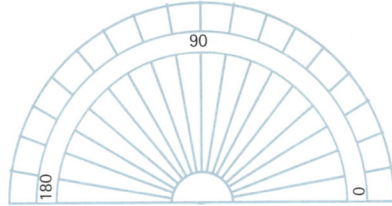

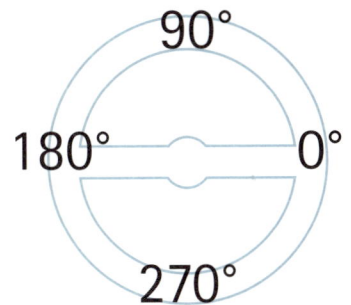

Use an angle measurer or a protractor to measure these angles.

90°
180° — 0°
270°

a)　　　　b)　　　　c)

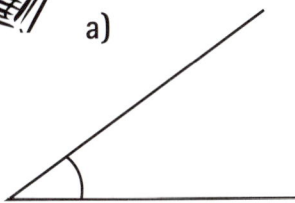

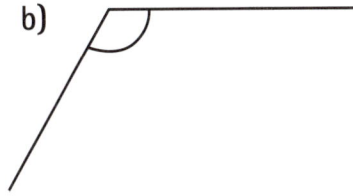

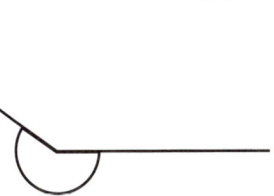

1 Read the question then read it again.

2 Use the curved line to help you find the angle you need to measure.

3 Study the angles.

Where will you measure? Use the curved line to help you.

Estimate and label the angles to help you check your answers:
(a) is an **acute angle** – less than 90°.
(b) is an **obtuse angle** – more than 90° and less than 180°.
(c) is a **reflex angle** – more than 180° and less than 360°.

4 Measure the angles.

Match up the angle measurer and the lines carefully.
90°
180° — 0°
270°

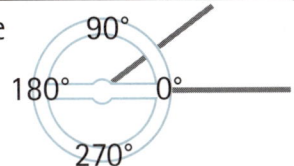

5 Check your answers against your estimates in Step 3.

Does each answer match your estimate?

6 If your answer looks sensible, write it in the box.

If not, go back to Step 3 and try again.

Drawing angles

Let's try drawing some angles. Use some paper to practise.

> Use an angle measurer or a protractor to draw these angles to the nearest degree.
>
> (a) 53°   (b) 87°   (c) 142°

1 Read the question then read it again.

2 Study the angles.

Label the angles to help you:

53° – an acute angle – less than 90°.
87° – an acute angle – less than 90°.
142° – an obtuse angle – between 90° and 180°.

3 Measure the angles.

Draw your first line (along the page). Then measure the angle you need. Draw your second line to join the first line at the correct angle you have marked.

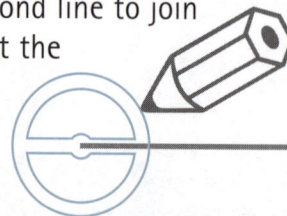

4 Check your answers against your estimates in Step 2.

Does each answer match your estimate?

To achieve Level 5 you also need to be able to measure or work out the size of the angles in a triangle and at a point.

Just remember: angles in a triangle add up to 180°.

Find the missing angles in these triangles.

(a) [ ]

60°   75°

(b) [ ]

90°

45°

55°

100°

(c) [ ]

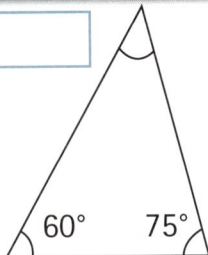

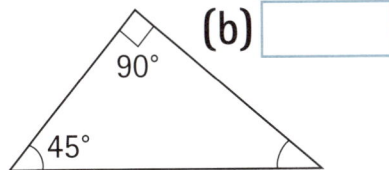

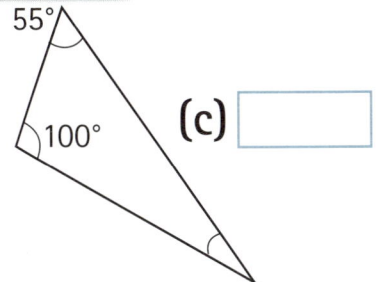

1 Read the question then read it again.

2 Picture the shape and remember the formula.

3 Study the numbers.

4 Calculate your answer.

5 Check your answer.

6 If your answer checks out, write it in the box.

We are given two angles. We need to work out the missing angle.

Angles in a triangle add up to 180°.

You know two angles so you can work out the third.

$60° + 75° = 135°$
$180° - 135° = 45°$

Add the three angles together:
$60° + 75° + 45° = 180°$

If not, return to Step 3.

Can you work out the remaining two missing angles?

★ Tip 1

Always turn the paper to make the angles easier to measure. Keep your measurer straight!

Make sure you read the correct scale.

90

180   0

★ Tip 2

Think of a darts board to help you remember the angles in a triangle.

One hundred and EIGHTYYYYY!

Angles at a point

Let's practise!

Calculate the angle at this point.

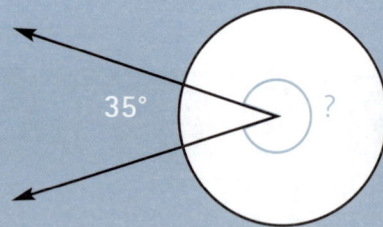

35°   ?

1. Read the question then read it again.

   Calculate usually means you need to do a sum to work out the answer!

2. Picture the shape. Estimate the angle.

   The angle is between 180° and 360°.

3. Remember the formula.

   A complete turn = 360°

4. Study the numbers.

   You know one angle so you can work out the other.

5. Calculate your answer.

   360° − 35° = 325°

6. Check your answer.

   Does it match your estimate?

7. If your answer checks out, write it in the box.

   If not, return to Step 4.

★ Tip 1

A complete turn = 360°

Imagine a skateboarder turning right around.

★ Tip 2

A right angle is always shown by a box.

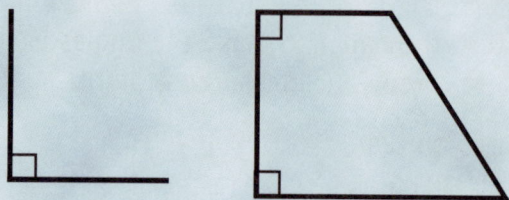

Practice questions

1 Find the missing angles in these triangles.

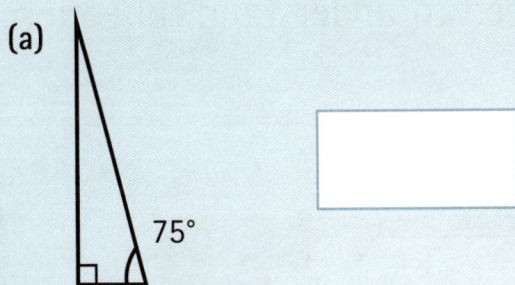

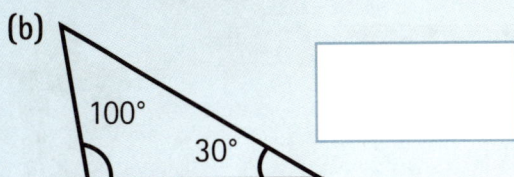

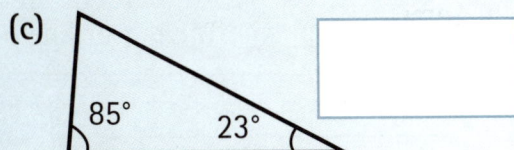

(a)

75°

(b)

100°
30°

(c)

85°   23°

2 Find the angle at each point.

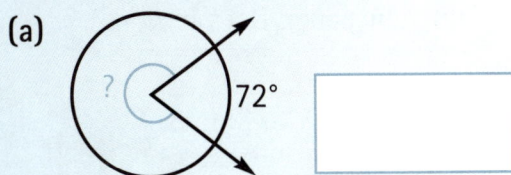

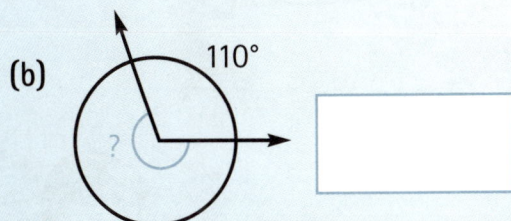

(a)

?   72°

(b)

110°

?

(c)

?

28°

3 Estimate the size of these angles. Then label them acute, reflex, obtuse or right.

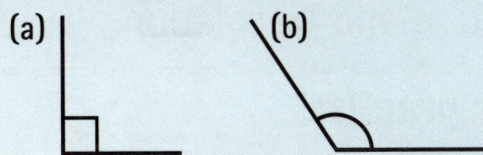

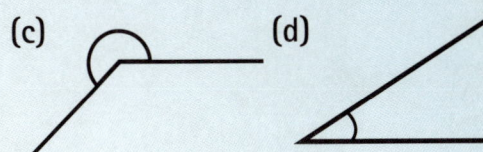

(a)   (b)

(c)   (d)

(a)

(b)

(c)

(d)

4 Draw an angle of 85° to the nearest degree.

5 Measure this angle to the nearest degree.

Symmetries of 2D shapes

Achieved?

To achieve Level 5 in Maths you will need to understand reflection, rotation and translation.

Let's practise!

Draw the reflection of this shape in the mirror line.

mirror line

1 Read the question then read it again.

2 Practise your answer.

Trace the shape and the mirror line onto practice paper.

3 Now complete the reflection.

Draw in the reflected shape on your piece of paper.

4 Test your answer.

Fold your paper. Does it work?

5 If it looks right, draw in your answer.

If not, go back to Step 3.

Does this shape have rotational symmetry?

A   B

1 Read the question then read it again.

2 Practise your answer.

Trace the shape.

3 Test your answer.

Rotate the shape 360°. Does the shape look the same in any other position?

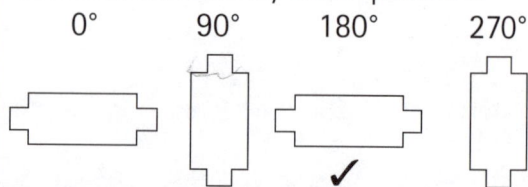

| 0° | 90° | 180° | 270° |

✓

4 Check your answer and write it in.

Yes. The shape looks the same as it does at the start when it is turned around 180 degrees! The shape does have rotational symmetry.

Let's try a question about translation now.

Sketch the position of the shape after a translation of 3 squares right and 4 squares down.

① Read the question then read it again.

② Practise your answer.

'translation' = slide along.

Trace the shape and practise before you write in your answer.

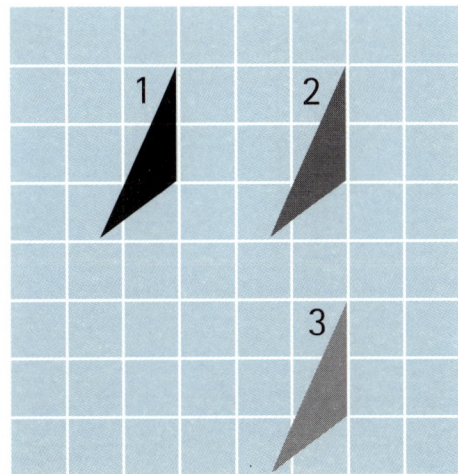

1   2

3

③ Draw in your final answer.

Double-check first.

★ Tip 1

If there is no grid given then trace the object and give it a base.

★ Tip 2

Translation means 'slide along'. It is not the same as rotation, which means 'turn around'.

Practice questions

1 Draw the reflections of these shapes.

(a)

(b)

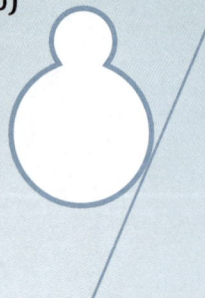

(c)

(d)

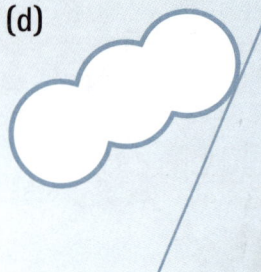

(e)

(f)

2 Which of these shapes have rotational symmetry?
Tick those that do.

(a)   (b)   (c)   (d)

X   T   ✿

Practice questions

3 Tick the correctly translated shapes.

(a)

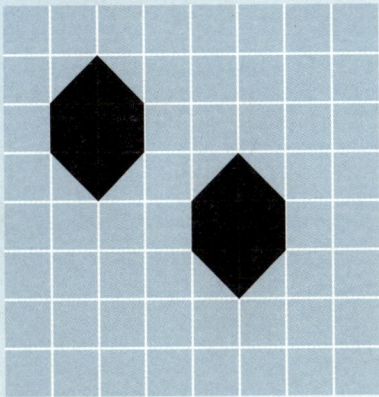

☐

(b)

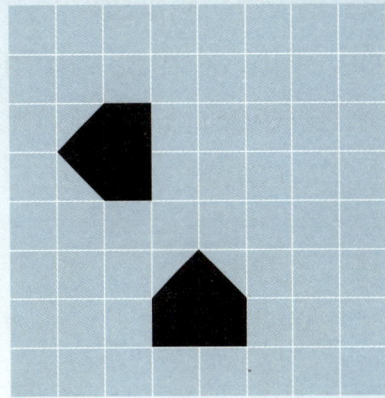

☐

(c)

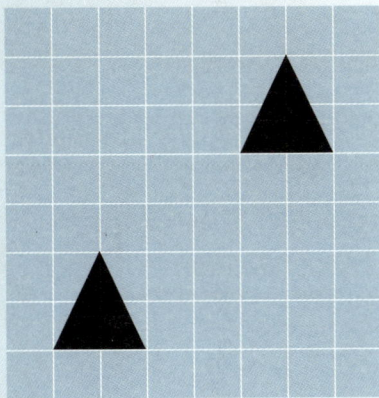

☐

(d)

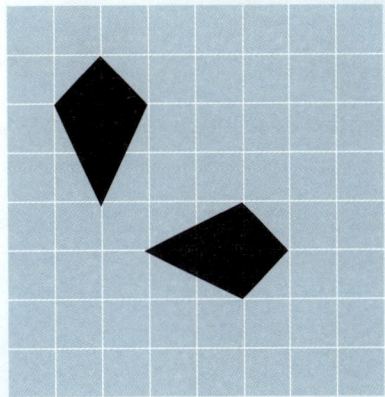

☐

(e)

☐

(f)

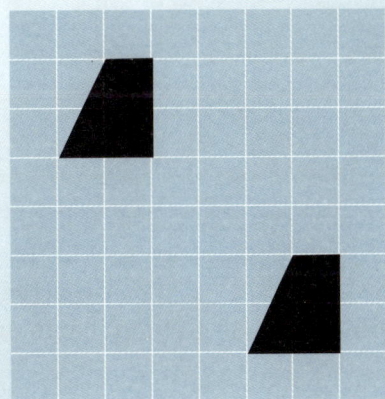

☐

★ Tip 1

Lines of symmetry = mirror lines

★ Tip 2

Don't let your paper slip!

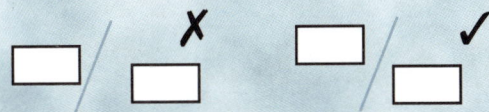

Units of measure

Achieved?

Comparing metric to imperial units of measure

To achieve Level 5 you will have to answer questions that ask you to compare metric units of measurement (kilometres, grams, litres and centimetres) with imperial units of measurement (miles, pounds, pints). Look at the conversions in the Key Facts on page 59.

Let's practise!

You run 3 miles to school each morning and 3 miles home each evening. How many kilometres do you run each day?

1 Read the question then read it again.

3 miles × 2 times a day = how many miles?

2 Study the units.

You run 6 miles each day. 1 mile is about 1.6 km.

3 Calculate the answer.

6 × 1.6 = 9.6

4 Remember the units you need for the answer.

9.6 miles

5 If your answer looks sensible, write it in the box.

If not, go back to Step 2 and try again.

Practice questions

Here are some questions. Use the Key Facts on page 59 to help you.

1 Approximately how many kilograms is 5 lbs of apples?

[ ] kg

2 I drink 1 litre of milk a day. How many **pints** of milk should I order from the milkman for a week?

[ ] pints

★ Tip

Revision rhymes!

A metre is just 3 feet 3. It's longer than a yard you see!

2 and a bit pounds of jam is round about 1 kilo of ham!

To achieve Level 5 you will have to answer questions that ask you to convert one metric unit to another metric unit.

Try this one.

Write 6.5 km as metres.

1. Read the question then read it again.

2. Study the units.

3. Calculate the answer.

4. Add in the correct units.

5. If your answer looks sensible, write it in the box.

6.5 km = ? metres

1 km = 1000 metres

6.5 × 1000 = 6500

6500 metres

If not, go back to Step 2 and try again.

Practice questions

Try some more questions.

1. The weight of my dog is 2.5 kg. What does he weigh in grams?

2. A nurse has a bandage that is 2.4 metres long. How many 30 cm lengths of bandage can she cut?

3. If I drank 1330 ml of water on Saturday and another 1330 ml on Sunday, how much water did I drink altogether?

Circle the correct answer.
(a) 8 litres
(b) 2.66 litres
(c) 13.30 litres

★ Tip 1

Make up some of your own questions to help you to compare units.

What would you prefer, 1 litre or 1000 ml of cola?

★ Tip 2

Measure things around you to get a feel for the different units.

g   or   kg

m

Estimating measures

Achieved?
☺ 😐 ☹

To achieve Level 5 you will have to estimate measures accurately. This mainly involves using common sense though, so don't worry. You will just need to think about length, weight and quantity in different amounts. These three questions are examples. The notes should help you with estimating.

> Suggest things you would measure in kilometres, metres, centimetres and millimetres.

★ **Kilometres** Anything or anywhere that is too far to walk! For example: the distance to the moon.

★ **Metres** Anything or anywhere that you could walk to or around. For example: the garden, playground or bedroom.

★ **Centimetres** Anything you could step over. For example: books, TVs or cereal packets.

★ **Millimetres** Anything you could step on and squash! For example: ants, Smarties or peanuts.

> Suggest things you would measure in tonnes, kilograms and grams.

★ **Tonnes** Anything you and your friends couldn't lift. For example: a ship, an aeroplane or an elephant!

★ **Kilograms** Anything you and an adult could lift. For example: a table, your friend, the sofa.

★ **Grams** Anything you could hold in the palm of your hand. For example: a gerbil, a tennis ball.

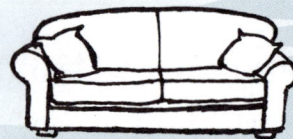

> Suggest things you would measure in litres, centilitres and millilitres.

★ **Litres** Anything that is too much for you to drink. For example: the bath, a swimming pool.

★ **Centilitres** Anything you might drink if you were thirsty. For example: a mug of tea, a glass of milk.

★ **Millilitres** Anything that is just a mouthful. For example: a teaspoon of medicine, a sachet of ketchup.

★ Tip

Get used to thinking about measures and remember a few standard ones to compare against others.

100 m = the length of a football pitch
1 kg = a bag of sugar
1 litre = a carton of juice

Then think about these:

50 m = $\frac{1}{2}$ the length of a football pitch
20 kg = 20 bags of sugar
100 litres = 100 cartons of juice

Picture them in your head.

Practice questions

1 Estimate the lengths of the following items. Then measure them.
Include the unit of measurement you are using.

Item	Estimated length (with unit)	Actual length (with unit)
(a) Your maths book		
(b) Your table		
(c) Your classroom		
(d) Your playground		

2 Which unit of measurement would you use to measure the following?

(a) The weight of a microwave oven

(b) The distance from London to Paris

(c) The amount of water in a garden pond

(d) The weight of an egg

(e) The length of a grain of rice

(f) The amount of cola in a glass

(g) The weight of a double-decker bus

(h) The length of a tennis court

(i) The amount of juice squeezed from an orange

KEY FACT - Measures

You may come across a question such as this.

Question: Suggest how you could measure the thickness of one sheet of paper.

This question is trying to catch you out but don't worry! All you have to do is to measure a large pile of paper and divide the total thickness by the number of pieces of paper in the pile.

So...

100 sheets of paper = 75 mm thick
75 ÷ 100 = 0.75 mm
Each sheet of paper is 0.75 mm thick

The area of a rectangle

Hurray! There is an easy way to remember how to answer questions about the area of rectangles. Just remember this formula:

Area of a rectangle = the length × the width.

Let's practise!

Find the area of this rectangle.

50 cm

29 cm

1 Read the question then read it again.

TAKE NOTE: you are working with AREA, so you need a formula!

2 Remember your formula.

The area of a rectangle = the length x the width.

3 Picture the numbers. What do they look like?

29 cm is almost 30 cm. Use this to estimate the answer.

4 Study the numbers again and think about them.

You can estimate that the answer should be around 1500. (50 × 30 = 1500)

5 Calculate your answer.

$$\begin{array}{r} 50 \\ \times \quad 29 \\ \hline 450 \\ 1000 \\ \hline 1450 \end{array}$$

6 Add in your unit of measurement.

cm squared (cm^2)   1450 cm^2

7 Check your answer against your estimate in Step 4.

1450 is close to 1500.

8 If your answer looks sensible, write it in the box.

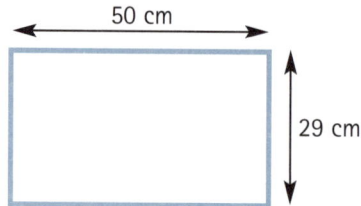

If not, go back to Step 4 and try again.

★ Tip 1

When dealing with area, make sure the units are ALWAYS squared.

e.g.   cm^2 m^2 km^2

★ Tip 2

Break up complicated shapes into smaller rectangles to make the question easier to answer. Remember to add up the areas of all the rectangles to get your answer!

Let's try another question. Here is a shape you will have to divide up into smaller shapes.

Find the area of this shape.

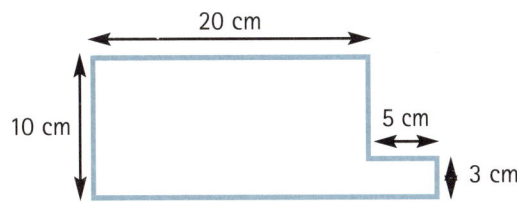

20 cm

10 cm

5 cm

3 cm

1 Read the question then read it again.

Look for the key words: **area** and **shape**.

2 Picture the shape.

It looks like two rectangles joined together!

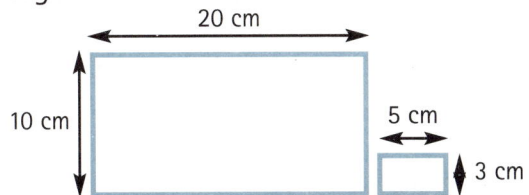

20 cm

10 cm

5 cm

3 cm

3 Remember the formula.

The area of a rectangle = the length × the width.
We need to measure two rectangles.

4 Find the areas of the two rectangles. Then add them together.

20 × 10 = 200
5 × 3 = 15
Total = 215

5 Add in your unit of measurement.

215 cm²

6 If your answer looks sensible, write it in the box.

If not, go back to Step 4 and try again.

Practice questions

Try some more questions.

1 Find the area of this shape.

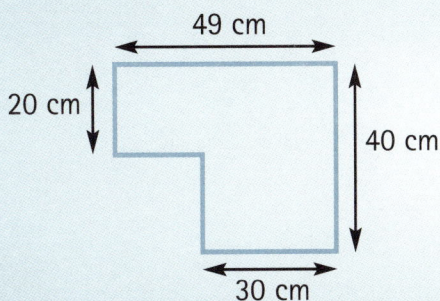

49 cm

20 cm

40 cm

30 cm

2 Find the area of this shape.

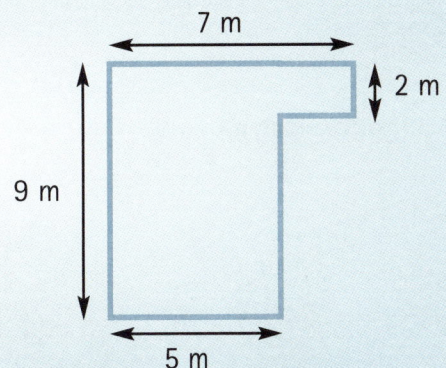

7 m

2 m

9 m

5 m

Finding the mean

Mean data is not 'nasty data'! You will need to be able to find the mean of a group of figures to achieve Level 5. Let's try a question.

Just remember: mean = average.

Find the mean of these lengths.

60 cm   28 cm   24 cm   51 cm   17 cm

1 Read the question then read it again.

'mean' = average

2 Think about the question.

Mean – add up the group of numbers and divide by how many numbers there are in the group.

3 Study the numbers.

You know your answer will be less than 60 cm (the longest) and more than 17 cm (the shortest). There are 5 different lengths.

4 Calculate your answer.

$60 + 28 + 24 + 51 + 17 = 180$
$180 \div 5 = 36$

5 Add in the unit of measurement.

36 cm

6 If your answer looks sensible, write it in the box.

If not, go back to Step 3 and try again.

Practice questions

Find the mean of these sets of numbers.

1 7, 7, 3, 4, 5, 10

2 25, 34, 36, 21, 18, 10

3 102, 93, 81, 84

4 16, 19, 21, 31, 42, 87

★ Tip

To find the mean:
Think about sweets! Don't be MEAN!
Share your sweets fairly! Add them all up then divide them equally!

Finding the median

To achieve a Level 5 you will need to be able to find the median of a group of figures too.

Just remember: median is the middle number in a group.

Look at these temperatures and find the median.

30°C, 10°C, –4°C, 12°C, 28°C, 23°C, 15°C

The median number is [   ]

1 Read the question then read it again.

2 Think about the question.

Median is the **middle** number in the group.

○○○○○○○

3 Picture the numbers.

Put them in order from lowest to highest: –4, 10, 12, 15, 23, 28, 30

4 Study the numbers and work out the answer.

15 is the middle number in this set of numbers.

5 Add in the unit of measurement.

15°C

6 If your answer looks sensible, write it in the box.

If not, go back to Step 4 and try again.

Practice questions

1 These are the ages of everyone in my family:
36 years, 7 years, 21 years, 10 years, 42 years

What is the median age? [   ]

2 These are the scores out of 20 for my maths group's mental arithmetic test:
11, 19, 13, 20, 18

What is the median score? [   ]

★ Tip

To remember **median** think **medium**
Small   **Medium**   Large
(Median is in the middle!)

Finding the range

To achieve Level 5 you will need to find the range of a series of data.

Just remember: the range is the difference between the lowest and highest value.

Let's practise!

These are the times 4 children take to get to school each day: 20 minutes, 1 hour and 30 minutes, 1 hour and 35 minutes, 45 minutes.

What is the range of these times?

1 Read the question then read it again.

2 Think about the question.

3 Picture the numbers.

4 Study the numbers.

5 Calculate your answer.

6 If your answer looks sensible, write it in the box.

The **range** is the difference between the **lowest** and **highest** value.

Put them in order: 20, 45, 1hr 30 and 1hr 35.

The longest time is 1 hour 35 minutes. The shortest time is 20 minutes. What is the difference between these times?

1hr 35 minutes – 20 minutes = 1hr 15 minutes.

If not, go back to Step 3 and try again.

Practice question

London Zoo has many visitors. What was the range of visitors for the 1st half of last year?

| January | 20 311 | February | 28 700 | March | 56 462 |
| April | 15 000 | May | 34 225 | June | 62 879 |

★ Tip

When calculating the range ALWAYS write down the numbers again, in order of size.

Finding the mode

Achieved?

To achieve Level 5, you need to be able to answer questions on mode.

Just remember: mode is another name for most common value.

Let's practise!

These are the results of the red group's maths test:

65, 65, 80, 72, 80, 80, 91

What is the mode?

1. Read the question then read it again.

2. Think about the question.

3. Picture the numbers.

4. Double-check.

5. Decide on your answer.

6. If your answer looks sensible, write it in the box.

The **mode** is another name for the most **common value**.

Make sets of the same number.

| 65 65 | 72 | 80 80 80 | 91 |

Make sure you haven't missed any numbers.

80 occurs most often.
80 **is the mode**.

If not, go back to Step 3 and try again.

Practice question

The children in Class 4 gave marks out of 10 for a particular television programme. These were the marks given:

6.5, 8.9, 3.9, 8.9, 7.2, 3.5, 6.5, 3.9, 6.5, 4.9, 7.2, 4.9, 8.9,
6.5, 3.9, 3.5, 6.5, 7.2, 8.9, 6.5

What was the mode? Mode =

★ Tip 1

Remember:
Mode is the **M**ost **C**ommon **V**alue
Modal means **Mode**

★ Tip 2

Always write out the numbers again and sort them.

Tick off each number so you know you haven't missed any of them. This is IMPORTANT!

Graphs and pie charts

Achieved? ☺ 😐 ☹

To get a Level 5 you will need to look at graphs like the one below and answer questions about them.

Let's practise!

These road signs are in miles. Use the conversion graph to rewrite the road signs in kilometres.

Dover 15 miles   Dover [   ] km

Canterbury 35 miles   Canterbury [   ] km

Hastings 45 miles   Hastings [   ] km

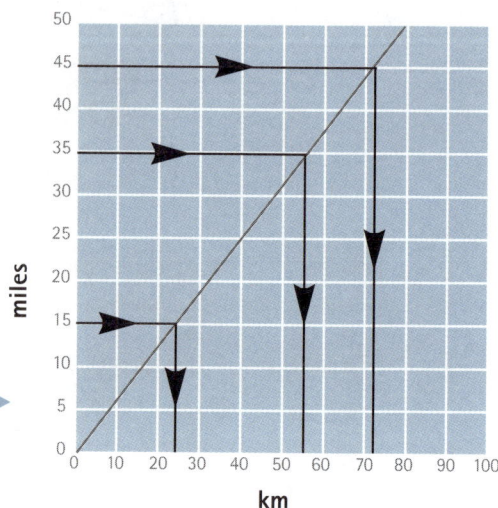

1 Read the question then read it again.

Conversion graph tells us that we need to convert values.

2 Be methodical.

Dover
- We need to change 15 miles into kilometres.
- Go up the y axis (miles) and find 15 (halfway between 10 and 20).
- Mark this point on the y axis with your pencil.
- Go across to the conversion line and make another mark.
- Now go down to find out the value in kilometres.

Our answer is 24!
Now repeat for Canterbury and Hastings.

3 Does the answer look sensible? If so, fill in the answer box.

Check your answers carefully on the graph before writing them in the boxes. The test marker is looking for an EXACT answer.

Practice question

The exchange rate for pounds to euros is £1 = €1.6. Using the graph above to help you, draw a new graph to convert pounds to euros. Use the graph to find out how much you would receive when you exchange:

(a) £15 = € [   ]

(b) £35 = € [   ]

(c) €40 = £ [   ]

(d) €64 = £ [   ]

Pie charts are a way of showing ideas as a fraction, percentage or proportion. They are an excellent way of showing information quickly and clearly... as long as you know what to look for!

Here are a few to remember:

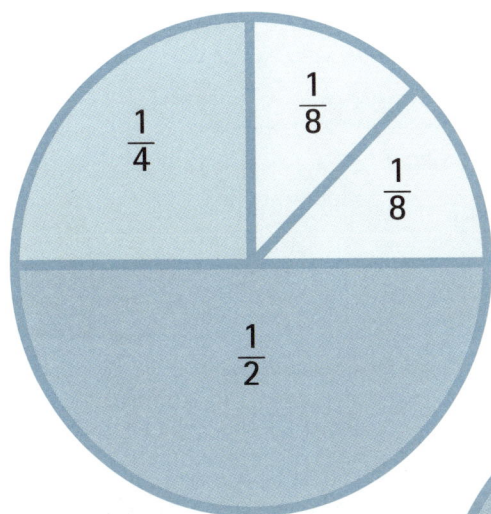

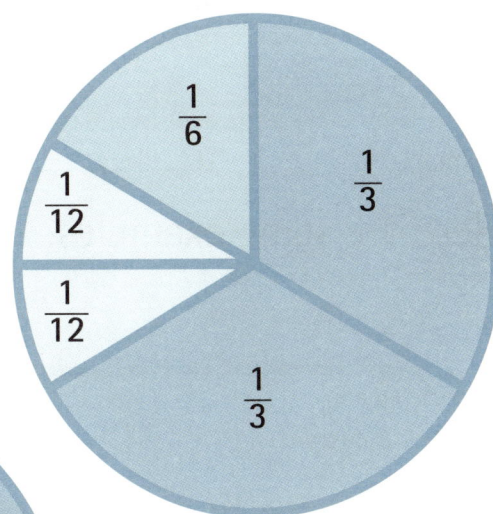

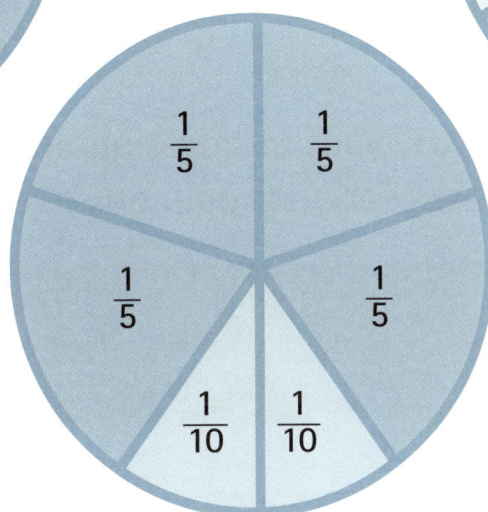

Practice questions

Use the pie charts above to estimate what fraction of the population of Kingston is:

a) 16 or under? b) 60 or over?

Ages of the population of Kingston

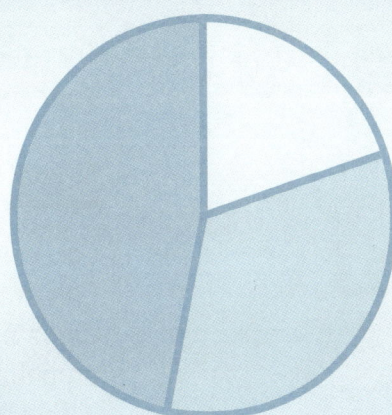

☐ 60 and over

☐ 16 and under

☐ between 16 and 60

★ Tip 1

Be VERY careful when reading scales or axes. You may be asked to find values BETWEEN lines on the scale. A test marker would want to know if you can find the EXACT answer.

★ Tip 2

Always draw graphs and read graphs carefully and accurately.
A sharp pencil, straight ruler and steady hand are essential!

The probability scale

The probability scale is a way of showing how likely something is to happen on a scale of 0 to 1.

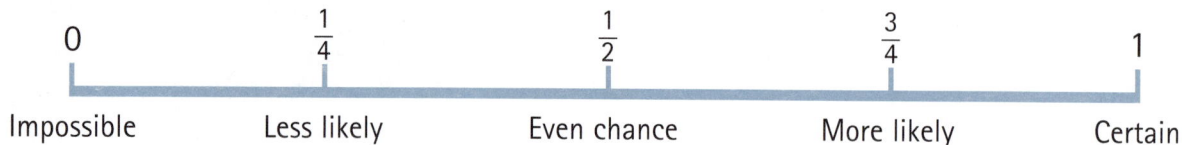

0	$\frac{1}{4}$	$\frac{1}{2}$	$\frac{3}{4}$	1
Impossible	Less likely	Even chance	More likely	Certain

Here are some examples:

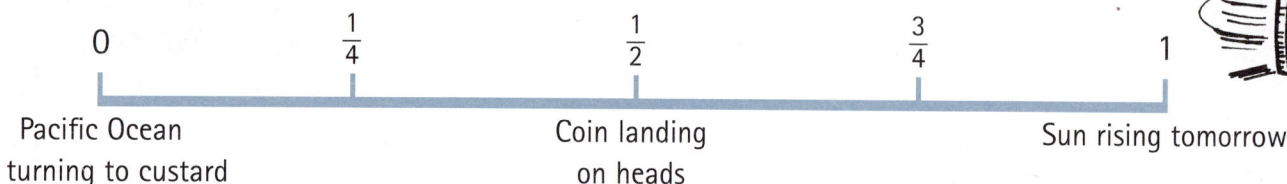

Pacific Ocean turning to custard — Coin landing on heads — Sun rising tomorrow

You will have to answer two types of question about probability scales. Let's try a question that asks for your opinion.

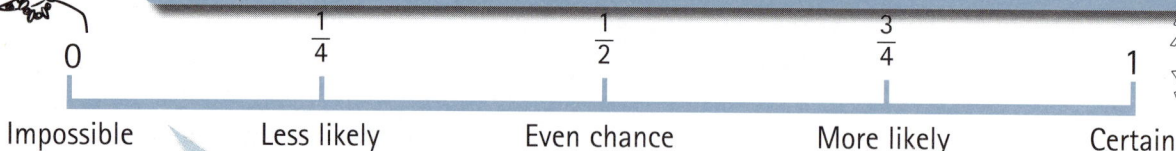

Place this statement on the scale using an arrow and a label.

'It will snow on Christmas Day this year.'

0	$\frac{1}{4}$	$\frac{1}{2}$	$\frac{3}{4}$	1
Impossible	Less likely	Even chance	More likely	Certain

1 Read the question then read it again.

Important here as there are more words than numbers!

2 Picture the question in your mind.

Try to imagine snow on Christmas Day. Your first thought might be: 'Yes that is likely because it's cold and Christmas is in winter.'

3 Picture the question again.

Can you remember any white Christmases? If you can then it is probably more likely. If not, then it's probably less likely.

4 Does the answer look sensible? If so, place your arrow on the scale.

Place your arrow on the scale pointing towards 'less likely'.

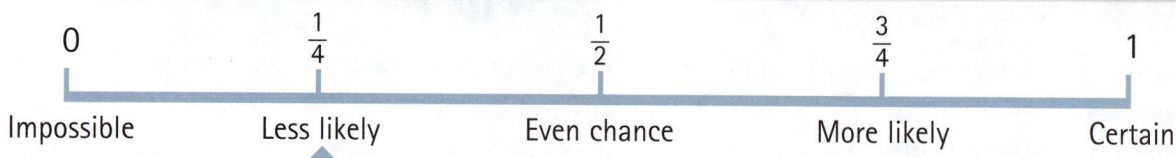

0	$\frac{1}{4}$	$\frac{1}{2}$	$\frac{3}{4}$	1
Impossible	Less likely	Even chance	More likely	Certain

'It will snow on Christmas Day'

Now let's try a probability question that asks for a mathematically correct answer.

These coloured balls were placed in a bag:

12 red   1 green   5 orange   2 blue

Estimate the chance that the first ball to be taken out of the bag will be an orange ball and mark it on the probability scale.

1 Read the question then read it again.

Words and numbers to think about. What is the question asking you to do?

2 Picture the question in your mind.

Try to picture the different coloured balls going into the bag.

3 Add up the total number of balls.

$12 + 1 + 5 + 2 = 20$

4 How many of them are orange?

There are 5 orange balls. So there are 5 orange balls out of 20.

5 Express your probability as a fraction, decimal or percentage. This is important!

This can be expressed as a fraction, percentage or decimal.

$\frac{1}{4}$ 25%   0.25

6 Decide where to place your arrow.

Draw the arrow a quarter of the way along the line. Be accurate here because the probability scale is clearly marked.

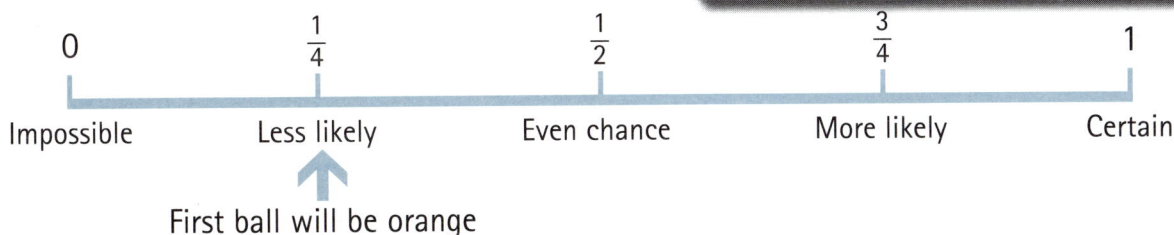

0	$\frac{1}{4}$	$\frac{1}{2}$	$\frac{3}{4}$	1
Impossible	Less likely	Even chance	More likely	Certain

First ball will be orange

Practice question

There are 24 beads in a bag. 6 are green, 6 are purple, 4 are brown and the rest are blue.
What are the chances of taking out a blue bead?
(a) Write your answer down as a fraction, decimal or percentage.
(b) Draw an arrow on this probability scale as an estimate.

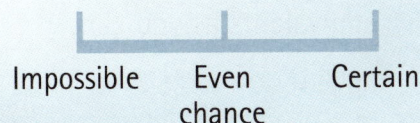

Impossible   Even chance   Certain

★ Tip 1

When throwing a dice there is an EQUAL chance of rolling any of the numbers.
When tossing a coin there is an EQUAL chance of getting heads or tails.

★ Tip 2

If you are not marking a probability on a scale you must present it as a **fraction, decimal** or **percentage**.

KEY FACTS

The Number System and Calculations

Multiplying decimals by 10, 100 and 1000
- Shuffle numbers to the left.
- Shuffle numbers to the left once when × 10, twice when × 100 and three times when × 1000.

Dividing decimals by 10, 100 and 1000
- Shuffle numbers to the right.
- Shuffle numbers to the right once when ÷ by 10, twice when ÷ by 100, and three times when ÷ by 1000.

Negative numbers
- Integers are just whole numbers.
- When counting from negative up to positive or positive down to negative, **remember to count 0!**
- When counting on a number line, count to the right when adding, count to the left when subtracting.

Decimals to two places
- When rounding, remember 5 is up!
  6.785 = 6.79

Reducing a fraction to its simplest form
- If you are asked to find a proportion or ratio of two things or numbers you are being asked to find a fraction (in its lowest form).

Calculating a fraction or percentage
- Remember as many percentage/fraction equivalents as you can:

  $50\% = \frac{1}{2}$ $25\% = \frac{1}{4}$ $75\% = \frac{3}{4}$

  $33\% = $ nearly $\frac{1}{3}$ $66\% = $ nearly $\frac{2}{3}$

Multiplication and division (with decimal points)
- × and ÷ are opposites.
- Always estimate first. It will help you to get the decimal point in the right place if one is needed.

Checking your answers
- Inverse means opposite!
- Check addition by subtraction – and vice versa.
- Check division by multiplication – and vice versa.
- Use 'friendly numbers' when estimating: 2, 5, 10 etc.

Simple formulae
- **Talk** through the formula in your head. It will make it easier.

Brackets
- Always do brackets in equations first.

Coordinates
- Always read ALONG (x axis) and then UP (y axis).
- Always write (x) before (y) – (x, y).
- Quadrants work **anti-clockwise**.

3 o'clock to 12 o'clock	= Quadrant 1
12 o'clock to 9 o'clock	= Quadrant 2
9 o'clock to 6 o'clock	= Quadrant 3
6 o'clock to 3 o'clock	= Quadrant 4

Measures, Shape and Space

2D shapes

- Pentagon
  Pentagons have FIVE sides.
  Regular pentagons have FIVE EQUAL SIDES.
- Parallelogram
  A parallelogram is a RECTANGLE THAT
  HAS BEEN PUSHED OVER.
  Remember the opposite sides are the same length
  but parallel.
- Isosceles and scalene triangles
  An isosceles triangle has TWO EQUAL SIDES
  AND TWO EQUAL ANGLES.
  Picture an isosceles triangle as an arrow!
  A scalene triangle has THREE SIDES
  OF DIFFERENT LENGTHS and THREE
  ANGLES OF DIFFERENT sizes.
  When picturing a scalene triangle, think of SCALING
  A MOUNTAIN that has an easy way up or a more
  difficult side to climb!

Angles

- Acute angle = 0–89°
- Right angle = 90°
- Obtuse angle = 91–179°
- Straight line = 180°
- Reflex angle = 181–359°
- Angles around a POINT always add up to
  360° (a complete turn).
- The angles of a TRIANGLE always add up to
  180°.

Symmetries

- When drawing reflections, remember to keep
  the correct distance from the mirror line.

Metric and imperial conversions (approximate)

- 1 litre = 1.8 pints
- 1 kilogram = 2.2 lbs (pounds)
- 1 pound = 0.454 kg
- 1 mile = 1.6 km
- 5 miles = 8 km
- 1 foot = 30 cm
- 1 metre = 3 feet 3 inches
- 1 inch = 2.5 cm

Estimating measures

- Milli = very small
- Centi = small
- Kilo = big

Area of a rectangle

- Area of a rectangle = length (L) × width (W)
- Area is always units squared (cm^2, m^2, mm^2)

Handling Data

Pictograms

- With pictograms PICTURE = NUMBER
  e.g. ⍭ = 20 ice creams ⌇ = 10 ice creams

Mean, median, range, mode

- Mean = sum of all numbers divided by
  number of numbers
- Median = middle number in sequence
  (always write down in order first)
- Range = difference between highest and
  lowest number
- Mode = most common value

Charts and graphs

- Be careful and accurate. Use a sharp pencil.
- Pie charts are good for percentages,
  fractions or decimals.

Probability scale

- Always goes from 0 to 1 (you need
  fractions/decimals here).

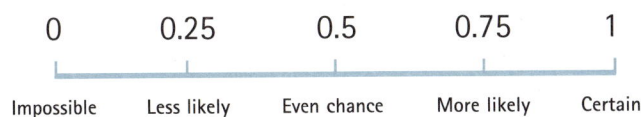

0	0.25	0.5	0.75	1
Impossible	Less likely	Even chance	More likely	Certain

Tips and technique

Before a test

1. When you revise, try revising a 'little and often' rather than in long sessions.

2. Learn your multiplication facts up to 10 x 10 so that you can recall them instantly. These are your tools for performing your calculations.

3. Revise with a friend. You can encourage and learn from each other.

4. Get a good night's sleep the night before.

5. Be prepared – bring your own pens and pencils and wear a watch to check the time as you go.

During a test

1. Don't rush the first few questions. These tend to be quite straightforward, so don't make any silly mistakes.

2. As you know by now, READ THE QUESTION THEN READ IT AGAIN.

3. If you get stuck, don't linger on the same question – move on! You can come back to it later.

4. Never leave a multiple choice question. Make an educated guess if you really can't work out the answer.

5. Check to see how many marks a question is worth. Have you 'earned' those marks with your answer?

6. Check your answers. You can use the inverse method or the rounding method. Does your answer look correct?

7. Be aware of the time. After 20 minutes, check to see how far you have got.

8. Try to leave a couple of minutes at the end to read through what you have written.

9. Always show your method. You may get a mark for showing you have gone through the correct procedure even if your answer is wrong.

10. Don't leave any questions unanswered. In the two minutes you have left yourself at the end, make an educated guess at the questions you really couldn't do.

The National Tests

Key facts

⭐ The Key Stage 2 National Tests (or SATs) take place in the middle of May in Year 6. You will be tested on Maths, English and Science.

⭐ The tests take place in your school and will be marked by examiners – not your teacher!

⭐ You will get your results in July, two months after you take the tests.

⭐ Individual test scores are not made public but a school's combined scores are published in what are commonly known as league tables.

The Maths National Tests

You will take three tests in Maths:

Mental Maths Test – This test will be played to you on a cassette. You will have to answer the questions mentally within 5, 10 or 15 seconds. This test will take about 20 minutes.

Test A – The non-calculator test. This test requires quick answers on a test paper. You will not be able to use a calculator but should show any working you do.

Test B – This test allows you to use a calculator and includes problems that will take you longer to solve.

⭐ Don't forget!

Using and Applying Mathematics – There will be more questions testing how you use and apply your mathematical knowledge in different situations. This includes: knowing which is the important information in the questions; how to check your results; describing things mathematically using common symbols and diagrams; and explaining your reasons for conclusions that you make.

Many of the questions include elements of Using and Applying Mathematics but we have also added extra pages with specific questions designed to help you succeed in this new area of testing: pages 48 to 59.

You might be asked to explain your answers and also write possible answers. Remember to always show your method.

Answers

LEVEL 4 TRICKY BITS

Page 8 – Predicting sequences
1) 55, 63   2) 0, –9   3) 67, 80

Page 9 – Calculators
1) 1308   2) 99.9   3) 80.25   4) 582.9   5) 2745.76   6) 10100

Page 11 – The 24 hour clock
1) 5hrs and 52 mins   2) 11hrs and 27 minutes   3) 6hrs and 46 minutes   4) 1hr and 45 minutes

Page 12 – Reading scales
1) 80 ml   2) 130 ml

LEVEL 5

Page 14 – Checking your answers
1) 3312   2) 1320   3) 594   4) 7485

Page 15 –   Checking your answers
1) 6248   2) 4212   3) 289   4) 46

Page 17 – Multiplying and dividing by 10, 100 and 1000
1) 370   2) 100   3) 3   4) 0.46
5) 10   6) 6.5

Page 19 – Decimals
1) 41.67   2) £6.14   3) 79.04   4) £20.15

Page 20 – Reducing fractions
1) $\frac{1}{3}$ 2) $\frac{3}{8}$ 3) $\frac{3}{4}$ 4) $\frac{4}{7}$

Page 21 – Ratio and proportion
1) 1:2   2) $\frac{1}{3}$

Page 23 – Calculating fractions or percentages
1) 375 cm   2) 64 kg   3) £91   4) 520 ml   5) 352 g   6) £999

1) 32%   2) 35%   3) 13%   4) 75%

Page 25 – Multiplication and division
1) 18   2) 71   3) 31

4) 12 635   5) 65 736   6) 12

Page 27 – Negative numbers

1) –7°, –5°, –2°, 0°, 3°

2) –25, –21, –17, 6, 17

3) –23°

4) 15°

Page 29 – Simple formulae

1) T = £9

2) N = 5

3) P = £18

Formula A = (J × 5) + 4

Page 31 – Brackets

1) 10 842

2) 884

3) 10

4) 11

Page 34 – Coordinates

1) (–3, –2) = 3rd Quadrant   (–2, 1) = 2nd Quadrant   (1, 3) = 1st Quadrant

2) (1, 0) (2, –2) (5, –2) (4, 0)

Page 36 – Angles

(a) 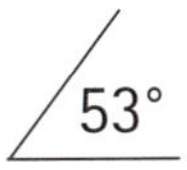 53°   (b)  87°   (c) 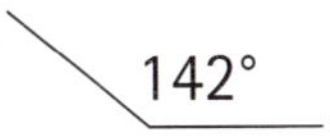 142°

Page 37 – Angles

(a) 45°   (b) 45°   (c) 25°

Page 39 – Angles

1) (a) 15°   (b) 50°   (c) 72°

2) (a) 288°   (b) 250°   (c) 332°

3) (a) 90° – right angle   (b) 135° (approx) – obtuse angle

   (c) 225° (approx) – reflex angle   (d) 45° (approx) – acute angle

4)

5) 55°

Page 42 – Symmetries of 2D shapes

1) (a)    (b)    (c)    (d)    (e)    (f)

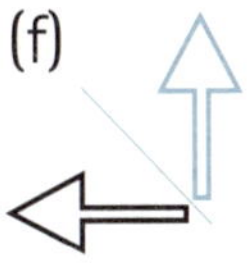

2) (a) ✗   (b) ✓   (c) ✗   (d) ✓

Page 43 – Symmetries of 2D shapes

3) (a) ✓   (b) ✗   (c) ✓   (d) ✗   (e) ✗   (f) ✓

Page 44 – Metric equivalents of imperial units

1) 2.27 kg   2) 12.6 pints

Page 45 – Metric equivalents of imperial units
1) 2500 grams   2) 8 lengths   3) 2.66 litres

Page 47 – Estimating with measures
1) (a) – (d) These will vary in estimates and actual measures dependent on your book, table, classroom and playground!
2) (a) kilograms   (b) kilometres   (c) litres   (d) grams   (e) millimetres
    (f) centilitres   (g) tonnes   (h) metres   (i) millilitres

Page 49 – Finding the area of a rectangle
1) 1580 cm^2 2) 49 m^2

Page 50 – Finding the mean
1) 6   2) 24   3) 90   4) 36

Page 51 – Finding the median
1) 21 years   2) 18

Page 52 – Finding the range
Range of visitors = 47 879 visitors

Page 53 – Finding the mode
Modal mark = 6.5

Page 54 – Interpreting graphs and pie charts
(a) €24   (b) €56   (c) £25   (d) £40

Page 55 – Interpreting graphs and pie charts
(a) $\frac{1}{3}$ (b) $\frac{1}{5}$

Page 57 – Probabilities
(a) $\frac{1}{3}$ or 0.33 or 33.33%   (b)

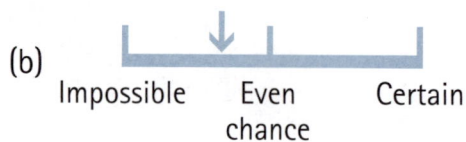

Impossible   Even   Certain
chance